BEFORE IT'S TOO LATE

HELP FOR WOMEN IN CONTROLLING OR ABUSIVE RELATIONSHIPS

Robert J. Ackerman, Ph.D.
and
Susan E. Pickering

Health Communications, Inc.
Deerfield Beach, Florida

A previous version of this book was published as *Abused No More*.

Publisher: Health Communications, Inc.
       3201 S.W. 15th Street
       Deerfield Beach, Florida 33442-8190

*. . . to the women who were willing to share part of their lives,
to help other women get through part of theirs*

Contents

PREFACE

One sees that dead, vacant look steal over the rarest, finest of women's faces . . . in the very midst, it may be, of their warmest summer's day; and then one can guess at the secret of intolerable solitude that lies hidden beneath the delicate laces and the brilliant smile.

—Rebecca Harding Davis

Knowing when to detach yourself from an unhealthy situation can be a healthy response. However, waiting too long can be dangerous. Too many women have paid the price for delaying. Newspapers are full of reports about crimes against women by an abusive partner. Certainly help is available, but it is not that simple. Getting out of any relationship is difficult. Getting out of an overly controlling one may seem impossible. However, many women are beginning to realize that alternatives are available, that change can happen in their lives—in or out of their relationships—and that living in fear is not living.

Abusive or controlling relationships produce fear. The more the fear grows, the harder it is to make rational choices. Once a relationship has passed the point of working things out, it usually deteriorates rapidly. Partners no longer trust each other, tempers run out of control, self-defeating behaviors increase and both partners begin to question their sanity and reasons for getting into the relationship in the first place. This is especially true for those living with very controlling partners, such as in the case of various types of abuse.

Living with someone who abuses you, abuses others or abuses substances is no spectator event. You cannot help but be involved. If you or someone you love is experiencing physical, sexual, emotional or spiritual abuse in a relationship, then this book is for you.

Not all abused women react alike. We know that many abused women try desperately to find a way to stop it; they confide in family or friends, turn to agencies for help, yet still they feel trapped, without hope and without a healthy means of recovery. We know that if her search for help fails, if the problem persists and grows, a woman begins to feel completely helpless. Not knowing what to do about the abuse and not knowing what to do about your recovery can be overwhelming. This is especially true for the many women in multiple or double jeopardy abusive situations. These are abused women who are involved with someone who also abuses alcohol, thus compounding the problem.

Unfortunately, abusing alcohol and abusing women are often correlated. The exact nature of the relationship between the two is seldom understood. Does one cause the other? Do both behaviors stem from something else? Regardless of the answer, we know two things. First, far too often the two forms of abuse occur together. Second, many women are in agonizing pain as a result.

In this book, we have sought to provide a unique look at the destructive interrelationship between alcohol abuse and spouse abuse. We disclose the type of information the abused victim must have not only about spouse abuse, but also about alcohol abuse. We recommend a combined recovery approach for the many victims of double jeopardy. Just as one is victimized by spouse abuse, so too is one a victim of its alcoholic component. Both of these victimizations require recovery to live a more emotionally satisfying life, free of denial, fear, depression, physical danger, low self-esteem, guilt, anger and hopelessness.

Our approach blends our experiences in two different fields to achieve one goal, recovery for abused women. Susan has worked for more than 15 years with abused women, as a counselor and group leader in women's shelters. Robert has 20 years experience in the alcoholism field, especially alcoholism and the family. Throughout this book there are many real case histories demonstrating the need for this combined effort. We hope that abused women will find insight, alternatives, growth, safety, health and the motivation to recovery in these pages.

Susan Pickering
Robert Ackerman

ACKNOWLEDGMENTS

We wish to thank all of the women we have met and worked with for sharing themselves and their stories. Without their willingness to give to others, this book would not have been possible.

We owe much to Judy Michaels for her ideas and chapter by chapter reviews, our appreciation to Edward Gondolf for his willingness to share his expertise on family violence, thanks to Lee Joiner and Pat Holiday for their suggestions and help, and finally, a very special thank you to Martha McNeill and Judy Sturges.

To the staff of Health Communications, and especially to Christine Belleris, Kathryn Butterfield and Kim Weiss for their help, many thanks.

To our greatest supporters, our families, and especially our spouses, Kimberly and Jerry, thank you.

Susan Pickering
Robert Ackerman

I

ABUSIVE RELATIONSHIPS

Before a secret is told,
one can often feel the weight of it in the atmosphere.

—Susan Griffin

Cathy was raised in an abusive family. Today, she is married and has three children. Her husband is very controlling and jealous. Cathy is abused by her husband, who promises he will stop.

The very first time it happened, I knew in my head it would happen again, but in my heart I wanted to believe that he would never hurt me. I loved him! The first time was around Christmas. I had just quit my job. We went out with my mother, her boyfriend and his son Jack. Everything was fine at first. I saw a friend of ours (my husband didn't like him) and went over to talk to him. When I returned, my husband said he was leaving and left me there. I was very upset and confused. Why would he do that? Jack took me home. Stan was waiting for me when I got home.

We started to fight, I got my keys and went for the door but he grabbed me before I could get to the door. He ripped the keys out of my hand and crushed my fingers. He whipped the keys across the room, grabbed me by the neck and threw me against the Christmas tree. I fell to the floor and he started choking me and bouncing my head off the floor. I was gagging.

Then he suddenly let go of me and went into the kitchen. He was very quiet and hung his head down. I lay on the floor for a few minutes and I was scared. I had never seen him like this before; he was a madman.

At first I thought he was going to kill me. That is a terrible feeling to have. I was sitting on the couch, and was crying and shaking. He came in and sat down beside me. He went to touch me and I jumped back.

He started to cry and told me he loved me and didn't want to lose me. He said he was so sorry for what he had done to me. I felt so hurt. I also felt guilty and sorry for him. I knew he loved me and didn't mean to hurt me. I believed him when he promised he would never do it again. I wanted to believe him so much.

In July, I was on vacation from my job. I asked Stan to take a day off so we could spend some time together. He looked at me and laughed and said, "For what?" That was the day I stopped loving him. I went into the house and cried. I felt like I was worthless and not important enough for him to take a day off for. His job came before me; everything came before me. Things were never the same between us again.

The second time was more frightening than the first. We went to a party at my sister's house. I knew something was wrong. He made mean, nasty remarks to me while we were getting ready. I was very upset even before we left for the party.

When we got there, I went to a corner and sat and was nervous. I was afraid he would get mad. He didn't talk to me for a while. Then he came over and I got up and we danced. I stayed with him all night and did not talk to another man for fear Stan would get mad if I did.

He got drunk and I wanted to drive home. Everyone at the party agreed, so he handed me the keys. In the car he started yelling at me, saying, "You think you're smart, don't you? You think I'm a dummy, don't you?" I didn't say a word.

He kept it up all the way home and I knew I was gonna get it. We got home and I jumped from the car and ran toward the house. He got to me on the porch, knocked me down and bit my lips. Oh, did that hurt. He knocked me through the door and hit me again and again. Oh God, why didn't he stop?

My daughter got up and I screamed, "My babies are up!" He knocked me down on Deana and then fell on top of us. I could hear my daughter screaming, "Mommy, you're hurting me." I kicked him off of me and drew my fist back and punched him with all my might. I was so mad that he had hurt Deana. Then he really started hitting me.

I ran to the phone but he grabbed it from me and smashed it. He fell to the floor and started to cry. I stood there watching him cry and begging me not to leave. I felt sorry for him but I also felt hatred for him for treating me that way. I was so confused. He begged me to stay and told me he loved me and would never do it again. These were the only times he would tell me he loved me.

I didn't know what to do. I didn't have any place to go and I really didn't want to leave my home. The next day Stan couldn't remember anything he did or said the night before. I asked him why he hurt me; he said he didn't know why. I couldn't understand him and I couldn't understand me for staying. I told him that if it happened one more time I was leaving for good. He promised me he would stop drinking and would never touch me again.

I didn't leave him the next time it happened. Each time he beat me, it got worse and worse. I put everything else in front of my needs as excuses for not leaving. We owned a nice home and had some nice things. I had worked hard to get what we had. My kids needed a father and I needed a husband to take care of me and the kids.

My own father had left us when I was real young. If I walked down the street today and he walked by, I don't think he would know me and I'm not sure I would recognize him, either.

Stan never laid a hand on the kids; if he had, I would have killed him. I kept begging him to stop drinking and stop hurting me and he kept promising, but he never did. Things were pretty bad between us. I avoided him as much as possible. I didn't sleep with him and avoided his advances; I couldn't stand to have him touch me.

One day we went to a wedding and I talked to another man. On the way home Stan was driving very fast and telling me to go get this guy because he had lots of money and that was just what I wanted. The more he yelled, the faster he drove. I pleaded with him to slow down, but he didn't. The kids were with us and they were scared, too. When we got home, he grabbed me by the neck and choked me and knocked my head off the walls. I'll never forget the look in his eyes. It's burned into my head: those eyes and their look of hatred.

When you think someone hates you that much, you don't feel too good about yourself. I thought I was a pretty bad person for him to hate me so much that he would beat me. Afterward he said the same things, but I had no feeling. I was just numb and empty.

I made him leave, but he came back in a couple of weeks. I felt this was his home, too and I felt bad for making him leave. I didn't want to leave and give up everything either. This was my home. I didn't know where to turn.

I pulled away from him because I couldn't trust him anymore. I was afraid all the time and felt I lived my life walking on eggshells. No one could help me. I wouldn't go near him and would not sleep with him. I made up excuses to not sleep with him. If he did something for me, he would always remind me and made me feel like I owed him. I felt like a whore. He had me believing that everything was my fault. He degraded me in front of my friends and in private.

One night he wanted me to go to bed with him and I started fighting him. He said he would rape me and I fought him off. He threw me on the floor and told me I wasn't worth it. It's confusing; I didn't want him to touch me, yet when he said that to me I felt cheap and ugly, like a whore.

One day I said to myself, "Is this the way you want to live the rest of your life?" My answer was, "No!" I gathered up my children and left the house. My husband told me, "Go! Get out of here, but you'll come crawling back to me."

Those words burned in me and I thank him because they helped me to stay away. At times when I feel weak and think I can't make it and should go back, I remember those words and they give me strength to stay away from him.

I went to a shelter where I received counseling and got back my self-esteem. I made some good friends there and learned that I wasn't the only one. I heard other women's stories and thought they were worse than mine. I met women in the group who had left and made it. "It was hard," they told me, "but you can make it."

I think back and wonder how I put up with it for so long. I always had a way of making myself very busy, so busy that I could block out all the bad stuff that was happening and not deal with it. I know now that I didn't really block it out; I just didn't deal with it.

After I left, I had nightmares for months. I could see those eyes and their look of hatred and I would wake up screaming and break into a cold sweat. It takes a long time to get over the fears.

My health suffered and my feelings about myself sank real low. I turned to drinking for solace. I never felt I had a drinking problem because when I left I didn't miss it at all or need it. But the drinking numbed me and kept me from doing something about my situation. I never told my counselor or the other women about my drinking, but now, almost a year later, I can admit it and see what it did to me at the time. I describe that part of my life as I look back on it as my being a wild horse and my husband trying to break me. He almost did break me, my spirit that is, but thank God I had enough spirit left to get myself out of there before I was really destroyed.

I'm living on my own with my three children. I am on welfare, have a job that pays minimum wage and, by the time I pay the sitter, there is not much left for us to live on. I'm going to get myself some schooling so I can get a better job. I miss my home very much and had to give up a lot of material things when I left.

I love my life now and I'm very happy. There are so many things to enjoy—a whole new world out there—and I want to enjoy it as much as I can. I will never go back to that life again; I can't. If I were to say one thing to other women reading my story, I would say, "Get out! It only gets worse. Where there's a first, there's always a second time."

ARE YOU IN AN ABUSIVE RELATIONSHIP?

It's regrettable that so many women can identify with Cathy's story. If you can identify with her physical, sexual, emotional or spiritual pain, then you may also be in an abusive relationship. It isn't easy to admit it. Regardless of the pain an abusive relationship causes, admitting its reality hurts emotionally. Still, Cathy's story does not reveal all the dynamics of domestic violence or its many faces. Some define domestic violence simply as the physical, sexual or emotional mistreatment of a woman by her husband, ex-husband, boyfriend, lover or companion. As we will show you, there is more to it than that. Domestic violence, spouse abuse, battered women, family violence and domestic disputes are all phrases used to describe the mistreatment of a woman by a man with whom she lives or has lived. Domestic violence can be considered a pattern of living. It is a pattern in which one member of a household uses violence and emotional abuse to gain control and dominance over the other members.

Violence is one method a male uses to keep a woman under his total control. To survive, she makes adjustments to this dominance. Resentment, hurt, anger, physical and emotional pain, low self-esteem and ruined lives accompany these adjustments. Abuse is a means for a single individual to consolidate and maintain power within the family or a relationship.

Abusive relationships take many forms and are not limited to physical abuse. In reality, there are no "pure" forms of abuse. Although we can identify and describe physical, sexual, emotional and spiritual abuse and neglect, it is our belief that abused women are always subjected to a combination of these. For example, all physical abuse involves emotional abuse. One may recover from the physical impact of being hit but, as with Cathy, the unanswered question "Why?" has lasting, emotional impact.

TYPES OF ABUSE

Abused women's case histories disclose several types of violence used against them. We see these repeated in case after case:

- Using weapons against them
- Twisting arms, tripping, biting
- Pulling hair, slapping, choking
- Beating, throwing them down
- Pushing, shoving, hitting
- Punching, kicking, grabbing

However, as we mentioned earlier, physical abuse is only one form of abuse against women. It is the one most apparent to others because of the noticeable physical consequences. Some of the not-so-apparent forms of abuse include:

- Intimidation
- Alcohol/drug addiction
- Emotional Manipulation
- Threats
- Sexual abuse
- Isolation
- Economic deprivation
- Using the children
- Using male privilege
- Rejection

Just as we know the types of abuse women experience, we also know their typical emotional reactions to the abuse. These are some of the feelings abused women experience:

- Powerlessness
- Hurt
- Guilt
- Shame
- Isolation
- Impaired trust
- Depression
- Helplessness
- Anger
- Humiliation
- Embarrassment
- Degradation
- Fear

Do any items on these lists ring a bell for you? Do you wonder if you are in an abusive relationship, or do you believe that your relationship is "just different"? Often an abused woman does not accept that she is abused and will contend that what has happened to her is not abuse. She makes excuses for his behavior and hers. Abuse cannot be rationalized or denied away. It can be hidden; it can be painfully endured; but it cannot be denied away. On the other hand, there are many women who know they are abused but haven't succeeded in stopping it. Either way, help is needed.

Once you realize abuse is present in your life, it is possible to

decide what you should do next. Stopping the abuse itself is a challenge. Recognizing and identifying the effect it has on you and your
children is part of the process of positive change. We can't fight or
conquer something if we deny its existence. Breaking through the
denial is essential to stopping the abuse. Recognizing and pinpointing
the types of abuse you have endured is a way to break through the
denial.

Once again, if you think you may be in an abusive relationship,
ask yourself these questions:

- Have I been hit?
- Am I losing confidence in my relationship?
- Is sex forced upon me against my will?
- Do I wish that he would drink less?
- Do I feel different from other people?
- Is my relationship unhealthy?
- Do I feel powerless and victimized?
- Are my children showing signs of the family turmoil?
- Do I feel that there is something wrong with me inside?
- Do I have a hard time taking care of myself, even though I care
  for others?
- Do I find it difficult to trust people?
- Do I feel lonely and isolated?
- Do I argue a lot about drinking?
- Do I feel used?
- Am I worried about my children's safety?
- Am I satisfied with my family relationships?
- Am I afraid to say "No" to his requests?

The more questions you answered "Yes" to, the more abusive your
relationship is becoming. Further questions might be, "How am I
affected?" "What should I know about abuse?" "What is alcoholism
and how does it affect my family and me?" and "How do I get help
for myself?"

AFTERTHOUGHTS

When we can't dream any longer, we die.

—Emma Goldman

*The easiest kind of relationship for me is with ten thousand people.
The hardest is with one.*

—Joan Baez

People change and forget to tell each other.

—Lillian Hellman

*Life's challenges are not supposed to paralyze you, they're supposed to help
you discover who you are.*

—Bernice Johnson Reagon

No woman can call herself free who does not own and control her body.

—Margaret Sanger

II

WOMEN IN THE CROSSFIRE

It is hard to fight an enemy who has outposts in your head.
—Sally Kempton

Women in abusive relationships are "in the crossfire." They are suffering not only abuse, but also many other negative behaviors. At the same time, they are maintaining numerous personal and family responsibilities. For example, abuse is almost always accompanied by controlling behavior and often is coupled with too much drinking. At the same time, if the woman has children, she must care for and support them. Additionally, many women are balancing an occupational career. All of these things put a woman in the middle of being "pushed and pulled." On one hand she is being bombarded by the abusive, controlling behaviors of her spouse, and possibly too much drinking as well. On the other hand she is being pulled to fulfill her responsibilities while trying to protect herself.

This tension often leads the woman to a concern for her own sanity and causes her to think and act in ways that impede her ability to help herself. Being caught in the crossfire leads her to an unhealthy identification with all of the negative things going on around her, while she is pulled to meet extraordinary demands. At this point she is usually overwhelmed and emotionally exhausted. Clear thinking gives way to emotional confusion, lowers self-esteem and creates a negative self-image; it is no wonder that self-defeating behaviors begin to develop.

Women who live with an addict or alcoholic are familiar with many of the crossfire outcomes. The condition is often referred to as co-dependency. But it doesn't stop there. Co-dependency is not limited to addicted families. It can also apply to any abusive family or any controlling relationship.

Robert Subby, an authority on co-dependency, defines it as "an emotional, psychological and behavioral condition that develops as a result of an individual's prolonged exposure to, and practice of, a set of oppressive rules—rules which prevent the open expression of feelings or the direct discussion of personal and interpersonal problems" (Subby 1987). Oppressive rules and living conditions are predominant features of both the spouse abuse and the alcohol abuse milieus. The common denominator of these two abusive situations is that both can produce co-dependency in those involved with the abuser or addicted person. This does not mean we believe that abused women cause their abuse. Co-dependency develops as a result of exposure to abusive conditions; it does not develop before these conditions.

CHARACTERISTICS OF CO-DEPENDENCY

All people may display co-dependent behaviors at one time or another, but that does not make them co-dependents. It is the degree to which these characteristics exist in a person that determines co-dependency. For example, the following would be typical co-dependent statements from a spouse in an abusive relationship:

"It's not that bad."

"I think it's getting better."

"It's just because I'm under so much pressure."

"I just do my thing; his behavior/drinking doesn't bother me."

"I never get angry."

"I'm not the type to go to treatment."

"I know I should talk to him, but it will upset him."

"He's really not an abuser; he didn't mean to hit me."

All these statements contain the most important ingredient of co-dependency: the language of denial. If you are going to be a "good" co-dependent you have to be in denial.

However, denial alone won't qualify you as a co-dependent. How many of the following statements apply to you?

- "I have an over- (or under-) developed sense of responsibility. It is easier for me to be concerned with others, even if it means ignoring my own legitimate needs."
- "I 'stuff' my feelings about my own childhood and have lost the ability to feel or express feelings because it hurts too much."
- "I am physically or emotionally isolated and afraid of people and authority figures."
- "I have become addicted to approval or excitement, and I have lost my identity in the process."
- "I am frightened by angry people and personal criticism."
- "I live as a victim."
- "I judge myself harshly and I have low self-esteem."
- "I am very dependent and I am terrified of abandonment. I will hold onto any relationship to keep from being abandoned."
- "I feel guilty when I stand up for myself."
- "I confuse love and sympathy, and tend to love people I can rescue."
- "I either have become chemically dependent, a compulsive

undereater or overeater, or have found in my relationships another compulsive person such as a workaholic, addict or abuser."

- "I am a reactor to life, not an actor."

Unrecognized co-dependent behaviors can keep you from getting help. Again, we do not believe that you have contributed to your abuse. Victims do not cause abuse. Women do not cause alcoholism in their husbands. People do not deserve abuse. You may, however, have co-dependent characteristics that not only keep you locked in dysfunctional relationships, but also keep you from "justifiably" helping yourself or your children. Many women expressed the following patterns about their relationships. Do any of these patterns sound like your present or past relationships?

- "I received little nurturing myself, and try to fill this unmet need vicariously by becoming a caregiver, especially to men who appear needy."
- "I was never able to change my parent(s) into the warm, loving caregiver(s) I longed for, so I respond deeply to the familiar type of emotionally unavailable men whom I can again try to change through my love."
- "Fearing abandonment, I will do anything to keep a relationship from dissolving."
- "I believe almost nothing is too much trouble, takes too much time, or is too expensive if it will 'help' the man in my relationship."
- "I am accustomed to a lack of love in my relationships and am willing to wait, hope and try harder to please."
- "I am willing to take far more than 50 percent of the responsibility, guilt, shame and blame in relationships."
- "My self-esteem is critically low; and deep inside I do not believe that I deserve to be happy or that I am as good as other people."

- "I have a desperate need to control my relationships, usually because of a lack of security in childhood, and I mask my control of people and situations by 'being helpful.'"
- "In relationships I am much more in touch with my ideal of how it could be than with the reality of how it is."
- "I am addicted to relationships and to emotional pain."
- "I am drawn to people with problems that need fixing, or I become involved in chaotic, uncertain or emotionally painful relationships, ignoring my responsibility to myself."
- "I may have a tendency toward episodes of depression, which I try to forestall through the excitement provided by an unstable relationship."
- "I find 'nice' people and comfortable relationships hard to identify with or be around."

Each "yes" affirms that for you, co-dependency is the over-identification with another person and the under-identification with, and under-development of, your own needs. It is as though every morning of your life you get up and ask, "Good morning; how am I?"

TOO MUCH CONTROL

Closely associated with co-dependency is being in a relationship with a partner who exercises too much control. The most common thing we have found among women in poor relationships is that they are in relationships with very controlling partners. Control can take many forms. The following is a list of common questions designed to identify overly controlling partners.

1. When there is a problem in your relationship, are you blamed by your partner?
2. Does your partner sometimes drink too much and become physically or verbally abusive?

3. Does your partner suspect that you have been involved with other people?
4. Is your partner usually late, or does he stand you up for appointments or dates?
5. Are you forbidden or criticized by your partner for having outside activities?
6. Are you embarrassed by your partner in front of other people?
7. Does your partner get angry when you disagree?
8. Does he accuse you of flirting when you were not?
9. Does he ever follow you to check up on you?
10. Does he criticize you for the way you look or dress?
11. Does he insist on driving the car all the time?
12. Has he ever hit you?
13. Does he do or say things to you that you never thought you would hear or experience?
14. Does he stop talking or withdraw affection when he doesn't win an argument or make a point?
15. Does he tell you he needs his "freedom" or "space"?
16. Has he pushed you or twisted your arm or used other physical acts to make you comply?
17. Does he forbid you to have your own checking account and then give you an allowance to pay the bills?
18. Does he use sex to quiet your relationship doubts?
19. Does he typically not show any interest in your day?
20. Does he give you extra money or buy you presents when you have been "good"?
21. Does he call you a nag or accuse you of stirring up trouble if you want to talk about problems in your relationship?
22. Does he often call you a demeaning or derogatory nickname?
23. Does he usually not phone when he is going to be late?
24. Does he want you around when he is home?
25. Has he been arrested at least once?
26. Does he feel angry or uncomfortable when you get attention?

27. Does he put down your accomplishments?
28. Does he trivialize or make fun of your feelings?
29. Do you often say he is too critical?
30. Does he ever flirt with someone else in front of you?
31. Does he ever make you feel sorry for him?
32. Does he ever frighten you with threats?
33. Does he find fault with your friends and people close to you?

If you answered "yes" to 20 or more of these questions you have a very controlling partner. If you answered "yes" to 12 or more you have a quite controlling partner. If you answered "yes" to 5 or more you have a somewhat controlling partner.

AFTERTHOUGHTS

We're all in this together—by ourselves.

—Lily Tomlin

*I have a right to my anger, and I don't want anybody telling me I shouldn't
be, that it's not nice to be, and that something's wrong with me because
I get angry.*

—Maxine Waters

*The non-liberated woman and the co-dependent are the same person . . .
she gets her identity completely from outside herself.*

—Anne Wilson Schaef

No one can make you feel inferior without your consent.

—Eleanor Roosevelt

Invisibility is not a natural state for anyone.

—Mitsuye Yamada

III

HE DRINKS A LITTLE,
HE HITS A LOT

---

*Women are afraid in a world in which almost half the population bears
the guise of the predator, in which no factor—age, dress or color—
distinguishes a man who will harm a woman from one who will not.*

—Marilyn French

No one likes to admit that her intimate partner has a drinking problem. We often hear spouses say, "He's not that bad yet"; "He can stop drinking anytime"; "He only drinks beer"; or "He doesn't drink any more than anyone else." Sometimes we hear defensive statements from the abused spouse, such as, "Why do you ask about that?" "Drinking has nothing to do with it"; or "It doesn't bother me." All these statements have one thing in common: denial.

Breaking through the denial of your spouse's drinking problem is easier once you fully understand how drinking causes problems, and that many of your problems stem directly from your spouse's drinking. The issue is clear-cut. How drinking and co-dependency interact to produce spouse abuse problems can be easily related. But if you are in denial, working through it can be complicated.

At the other extreme, some female victims are so accepting of a spouse's drinking that it practically becomes an excuse for his abusive behavior. Statements such as, "If only he didn't drink, everything would be fine"; "He is only abusive when he is drinking"; or "He's the nicest person in the world when he's sober" are often heard. Statements like these may be considered denial in yet another form: denial that the partner is abusive and accountable for his actions.

Whenever we hear statements like these, we know that the victim is in double jeopardy and experiencing twice as much pain as others. There is no such thing as drinking "a little" when drinking causes abuse. If drinking causes problems, then it is a problem.

ALCOHOL PROBLEMS AND SPOUSE ABUSE

When alcohol becomes part of a relationship, abusive patterns become even more complex and confusing—not simpler, as you might think. The widespread belief that a man abuses a woman because he is drunk is actually just one of many scenarios of abuse reported by women. The following examples are some of the patterns that may emerge when drinking and spouse abuse occur together.

USING VIOLENCE TO AVOID DRINKING OR USING ALCOHOL TO AVOID VIOLENCE

In this interaction pattern, the abuser may batter a spouse as a way of warding off a drinking episode, or he may drink to avoid becoming abusive. The idea that one of the behaviors can prevent the other from happening is erroneous. Abusive relationships are tension-filled relationships, and the tension in the home can become so unbearable that it is like a time bomb.

Regardless of which motive predominates, this rising tension usu-ally results in either the drinking or the abuse. Most often, both occur. Thus, the batterer who becomes extremely anxious and tense begins to drink to manage the stress. However, not only is he unable to control the drinking, but he also becomes abusive as he drinks more and more.

In a reverse flow of the cycle, tension leads to abuse, which leads to further anxiety, which leads to drinking. The man who practices this pattern is convinced that one of the behaviors can keep its counterpart from occurring. In reality, one of the behaviors merely precedes the other: violence before drinking or drinking before violence. Just as inevitably as the behaviors follow each other, the woman continues to endure the episodes, one after the other.

THE ABUSER DRINKS AND THEN BELIEVES HE HAS A LICENSE TO ABUSE

A "good" excuse for the abuser is that he was under the influence of alcohol and was unaware of what he was doing. Our society toler-ates many unacceptable acts committed by people "under the influ-ence" of alcohol. People are killed by drunk drivers who receive sentences of two to five years by pleading they were not in control but "under the influence" of alcohol. Barroom fights are seen as the guys "releasing a little steam" while "under the influence."

Society at large, and many abused women, are more likely to rationalize violence when an abuser is under the influence of alco-hol. This is an excuse that helps perpetuate the problem of spouse abuse. There is no acceptable excuse for violence. Both partners in a relationship need to contribute and receive love, acceptance, security, safety and understanding. Being a spouse with a drinking problem does not excuse a man from relationship responsibilities, and if you are the nonalcoholic spouse you should not excuse him either.

The Woman Drinks and Then Becomes a Target for Abuse

In a statistical profile of addicted women in treatment, a large midwestern women's treatment facility found that 44 percent of the addicted women treated had been battered (The Gables 1985). Women and alcohol addiction will be discussed more thoroughly in chapter 6.

The female alcoholic is at risk in many ways. Many of her problems, and often the abuse that she endures, are due not only to her alcoholism, but also to the attitudes of her spouse about women and alcoholic behavior. Quite simply, many men cannot tolerate alcoholism or drunkenness in women. Therefore, she becomes a target for his contempt and highly vulnerable, in her drunkenness, to his attacks. She cannot think as clearly, nor as quickly, if she finds herself in danger of being battered. Depending on how much she has had to drink, she may be unable to physically defend herself. The abuser may tell her she deserves the abuse because she's a drunk. And her guilt and shame may convince her that he's right.

Drinking May Occur Before, During or After Violence

Although an alcoholic's drinking may conform to a predictable pattern, his violence may not. Many alcoholics drink in cycles, such as on certain days of the week or month. Other alcoholics rely on a certain level of alcohol intake daily. Any of these patterns means that you must constantly be on guard for violent behaviors related to his drinking.

Creating even greater uncertainty, he may not be violent every time he drinks. This is not like living with a time bomb; this is living with an arsenal: You don't know when the fuse will be lit, or which fuse leads to another bomb.

The Abuser Who Drinks Seeks Treatment for Battering, but Continues Drinking

The drinker may not think he has a drinking problem, but accepts that abusing his wife is a problem. He gets help for the battering and stops the physical abuse, yet continues to drink. Although the physical abuse has stopped, the other forms of abuse continue. This is an unlikely pattern, though, since abusers who drink are more likely to seek help for the drinking problem first.

Consider the relative number of alcohol rehabilitation programs versus the number of battering programs. Programs for men who batter women are few and far between. Then, too, there is the matter of visibility. Battering is a more private problem than drinking because it usually occurs in the home. Few people are likely to witness the assaults. While drinking does occur in the home, it also occurs in other places where more people can witness the effects.

Many times, when the abuser is in treatment for battering, his alcoholism is neither detected nor addressed. There are several explanations for this. The abuser may not think he has a drinking problem and so he doesn't mention it. The spouse or family members may not be included in the treatment program or, if included, they may deny that he has a drinking problem. They may be unaware that there is an alcohol problem. Or they may fear bringing up the subject. Any of these scenarios can mask the alcohol problem.

THE DRINKING ABUSER SEEKS TREATMENT FOR ALCOHOLISM, BUT CONTINUES TO ABUSE

This pattern is the exact opposite of the one above. However, many of the reasons are the same. In alcohol treatment battering may not be addressed. The abuser may not consider it a problem. If the spouse or family is brought into treatment, they may fear bringing up this sensitive issue or hope that since he has stopped drinking, he will stop his abusiveness. While there is treatment for each problem, few treatment programs exist that address the two simultaneously.

DOUBLE TROUBLE, SINGULAR EFFECT

Alcohol abuse and spouse abuse are a complex and volatile combination. They often intensify each other and create a vicious cycle that is hard to break. Although alcohol abuse and domestic violence are two separate phenomena, they affect the family similarly. The following are characteristics, attributes and behaviors common to both problems.

DENIAL

The abuser and drinker deny or minimize their acts. They deny that the abuse or drinking occurred, or downplay its severity. The confused spouse wonders whom to believe, herself or him? She begins to doubt her own perceptions and also denies or minimizes what has happened.

BLAME

Both abusers and drinkers have strong tendencies to blame others for what they do. They find excuses. "If you didn't nag me so much, I wouldn't have gone to the bar"; or "If you had listened to me and done as I said, I wouldn't have had to hit you" are typical statements we hear. Neither the abuser nor the problem drinker wants to accept responsibility for his behavior. Instead, the spouse may accept the responsibility for it. Within herself there is a battle; she replays, in her mind, the scene of what happened, searching for answers. She is in a dilemma. If she accepts some responsibility for causing it, she must find ways to keep it from happening again. If she thinks that he was indeed responsible, how does she go about making him stop? Either way she looks at it puts her in the dilemma of trying to stop the abuse from recurring. She believes that in some way she should be able to control what he does.

ROLE CONFUSION

A Dr. Jekyll and Mr. Hyde personality is often displayed by an abuser. He acts like two very different people. He can be a caring partner one minute, a monster the next. The spouse reacts in disbelief: "This can't be the man I know and love." She may tend to disregard the actions of Mr. Hyde and think of him only as Dr. Jekyll. This is a form of denial. She may start to live in fear, becoming anxious and jittery, never sure of who he will be at a given day, hour or moment.

BROKEN PROMISES

The spouse abuser and alcohol abuser will both promise never to do it again. They can be full of remorse and very sorry for what they did after an incident. Both kinds of abusers try to regain control. These attempts create false hopes for all concerned. When it happens again, the guilt is compounded. It becomes a vicious cycle, with everyone who is involved feeling more and more hopeless as it spirals toward more and more destructive forms of abuse.

ROLE REVERSAL

The spouse abuser and/or alcohol abuser may expect his wife to act as his mother did. If his father drank or battered, and his mother tolerated it by doing nothing as seen from a child's eyes, then his wife should, too. The role he expects his wife to play is the same one he saw his mother play. A spouse may try to play this part or she may rebel. If she refuses to react the way his mother did, it makes him angry.

Sometimes the wife will go to her mother-in-law and tell her what is happening. From this, there are several possible outcomes. The mother-in-law may reply that she knows about it, but that the wife should stay because it is her role to keep the family together. She may offer interpretations such as, "You are the only one who can help him"; "He needs you and you can't just desert him"; or "He's acting like his father, and that's the way men act." She could ask, on the other hand, that the wife do something about it, such as getting outside help or leaving. She may even admit having always wished she had done something, but that she didn't have the strength, and hopes the daughter-in-law will do what she couldn't: get help or leave. The response a woman gets when she asks for help is crucial to what she will do next. The mother-in-law's response can either support the notion that she must play her husband's expected role or that she has the right to do something about it.

CONFLICT

Spouse abuse and drinking provide an unrealistic solution to conflict. In troubled families the most prevalent source of conflict is the relationship between the spouses. This relationship dominates all others. Unfortunately, attempts at developing alternative ways to handle conflict rarely go beyond either drinking or fighting. If the household is tense, and the wife threatens to make changes, the husband may use abuse to stop her. In a perverse way, the conflict has been resolved for the moment. The wife now must deal with the abusive incident and is no longer thinking about making changes. If the husband resorts to drinking, the wife concentrates her energies and attention on that problem. This type of conflict resolution, moment-by-moment, creates problems day after day for the wife.

GENERATION TO GENERATION

The most fundamental feature shared by these abuses, and those who endure them, is that they are passed from generation to generation. We know that alcoholism runs in families, and we know that abuse is passed on from one generation to the next.

CO-DEPENDENCY

Co-dependency, too, is transmitted across generations within families. If you identified with any of the characteristics of co-dependency and you are in an abusive relationship, it would not surprise us that you may have grown up in a family where one or both of the problems of abuse or alcoholism existed. These generational problems, which may have been passed on to you, may be the ties that bind you to a negative past, to a current abusive relationship and also to the trap of co-dependency. Co-dependency keeps its victims from developing the alternatives necessary to break these family cycles. You may not only be up against the abuse and alcoholism, but because of your family background you may be up against yourself. The true relationship between alcohol abuse and spouse abuse can go on and on and on until you break it, break it, break it.

AFTERTHOUGHTS

Before marriage, a man declares that he would lay down his life to serve you; after marriage, he won't even lay down his newspaper to talk with you.

—Helen Rowland

Am I like the optimist who, while falling ten stories from a building, says at each story, "I'm all right so far"?

—Madeleine L'Engle

It's usually the most wounded among us who inflict pain on others.

—Patti Davis

Life is a process of becoming, a combination of states we have to go through. Where people fail is that they wish to elect a state and remain in it. This is a kind of death.

—Anaïs Nin

Above the titles of wife and mother, which, although dear, are transitory and accidental, there is the title of human being, which precedes and outranks every other.

—Mary Livermore

IV

WHY DO I STAY?
LET ME COUNT THE WAYS

It occurred to me when I was thirteen and wearing white gloves and Mary Janes and going to dance school that no one should have to dance backward all their lives.

—Jill Ruckelshaus

The question most often asked about an abused woman is, "Why does she stay?" The answer lies in her uniquely personal perceptions and interpretations of her past and present. We can only understand why a woman stays with her abusive or alcoholic spouse if we consider the many factors that influence her life today, together with her upbringing. Among the critical elements that shape her perceptions are family, education, religion and community. The messages, values and attitudes that she develops toward herself; her opportunities, her life chances, her self-concept; and her attitudes or beliefs about appropriate and inappropriate female and male roles will greatly contribute to whether or not she remains in an abusive relationship. What she feels is affected by her present surroundings and how she interprets them too. The greatest influence, however, will come from her family background.

FAMILY BACKGROUND

Family background can inspire an abused spouse's "logic." What kind of chidhood did she have? What kind of role models did her parents provide? She may have been raised in a patriarchal system where the father was the powerful, controlling figure; where "What he says goes and everyone must obey." The mother, knowingly or unknowingly, may have reinforced this message. If her father abused her mother and the mother stayed, the daughter learned that a mother either had no other option or believed that abuse was something to be tolerated. The message passed down to the daughter: men are in control; you have no choices and you must obey.

In a matriarchal system, the mother is strong and powerful and takes care of everything. Here, the message that women are strong and can handle everything is passed down. Later, when the daughter finds she can't take care of everything and everybody, she may feel like a failure for not being "superwoman." In either system, patriarchal or matriarchal, messages that can directly or indirectly foster abuse are passed down to sons and daughters.

Some other familiar messages from parents are: "A woman's place is in the home"; "A woman stands by her man, no matter what"; and "You're going to grow up and find a man to take care of you."

A woman builds her repertoire of behaviors around the structural role models her parents provide. It is through these models that she first learns how men and women act toward each other. Three of the strongest messages she can receive, which increase the probability of her not only being in an abusive relationship, but also staying in one, are:

1. Those you love are those you can hit.
2. If her mother was abused and stayed, the message is that women have no rights and must endure whatever happens.
3. The woman is responsible for the success of a family or relationship, and it is her responsibility to stay.

These messages and others like them can place a woman at high risk. Emotionally-charged actions and reactions of family members serve as powerful teaching tools.

Family and other early influences on a woman are all predisposing factors. They occur before the fact. Negative predisposing factors place a woman at a high risk for an abusive relationship. Events and circumstances influencing why she stays in the relationship are called precipitating factors. These are the circumstances that surround her in the abusive relationship itself. Predisposing and precipitating factors can contribute to her staying, motivate her to seek help or motivate her to leave. Every woman in an alcoholic, co-dependent or abusive relationship will have her own reasons for staying. However, the following are the ones heard most often:

FEAR

Fear is a strong deterrent to resisting abuse or searching for alternatives. It can keep you from seeking change, especially if the result is uncertain. Many abused women live in fear of staying and yet still fear leaving, often just as much or more. Staying is a known condition that causes you to fear what you know can happen. Leaving, or searching for other alternatives, is an unknown that can cause you to fear the undesirable things you think may result.

JANE: A SEVERELY STRAINED RELATIONSHIP

Jane is a woman in her mid-thirties, a mother of four teenage children. She was in a second marriage to a man who had been in and out of prison for the last six years and on parole for the past 18 months. Their relationship was severely strained.

Jane had endured recurrent abuse, such as being knocked around, slapped, pushed, punched and threatened. Her husband forced one of her daughters, when he had her alone, to undress in front of him. The daughter was able to tell her mother, who bravely confronted her husband about the incident.

His reaction was to pull a gun and order her to leave the house with him, leaving her children behind. If she didn't go with him, they would all be shot. From the beatings she had endured she believed he was capable of carrying out his threat. She had been beaten by him and knew he could be cruel. Just how far he would go to carry out his threat was something she was not going to test, especially when the safety of her children was at stake. She saw no other choice; she went with him. Her fear caused her to do just as he ordered, even though it was against her wishes.

It would be unfair to say that Jane should have taken another action. She believed that she did the best she could. When it comes to personal safety or the safety of those we love, we all will do what we think is going to keep us safe. Unfortunately, staying and continuing to be abused damages her self-esteem, her relationships and her family. Probably most important is that threats can be more readily carried out if she is living with the abuser.

Threats play an influential role when women try to get away from their abusers. Men have threatened their wives with statements like these: "If you leave, you'll really get it"; "You think this is bad, just try leaving"; "I'll kill you before you can leave me"; "I'll hunt you down and kill you if you leave me"; or "I'll kill you, the kids, and then myself."

A woman's fears are real and justified. Sometimes these threats are carried out. Listen to the news and you will hear stories of wives who have been murdered by enraged spouses. Out of fear, abused women have been known to kill their husbands as a last resort.

There are other alternatives to this extreme outcome and the abused woman needs to know what they are. However, not only can fear keep you in an abusive relationship; it can also keep you from seeking alternatives. This occurs because you may fear reprisals if the abuser discovers you are looking for a way out, or because you fear what it will be like for you when you leave.

DEPENDENCY

The two most significant forms of dependency that keep an abused woman in a relationship are economic and emotional. Both of these, however, do not need to be present simultaneously. For example, an abused spouse can be negatively emotionally dependent or co-dependent, but financially independent. In another instance, the abused spouse no longer feels any emotional dependency on the abuser, but is unable to financially sustain herself, particularly if she has children. Finally, we know that the abused woman can experience both forms of dependency. When both are present, each seems to magnify the other.

When she is financially dependent, it is usually because of the presence of children. We know that regardless of whether it is a one- or two-paycheck family, any loss of income will alter the standard of living. Many women cannot afford this loss of income and still maintain an adequate or healthy standard of living for themselves and their children.

Emotional dependency is an emotional magnet. It keeps pulling you back. Trying to end a relationship is hard even on "peaceful" terms. In a negative relationship, the guiding principle is that a relationship that ends on a bad note never ends. Negative emotional dependency is the type of dependency experienced by abused women. Being positively dependent upon another for reciprocal love, caring and nurturing fits our nature. We all need other people in a positive sense to contribute to our well-being. Therefore, do not assume that dependency, in and of itself, is the problem. We can all be positively or negatively emotionally dependent.

A woman in an abusive relationship often expresses a "love/hate" feeling. She believes there are parts of the relationship or of her partner that still attract her; at the same time there are parts of the relationship that are absolutely destructive. These mixed messages further confuse the dependency problems. She wants to stay; she wants to leave; she believes she can do neither.

DENIAL

Denial is a defense mechanism you can use to ignore the reality of a situation or the need to leave it. Excuses for abuse can be offered to yourself and others in order not to focus on the abuse itself and the hurt that results from it. Denial runs through each of the following statements:

- "He didn't mean it."
- "He was under pressure from his job."
- "The kids were hassling him."
- "His father used to beat him."
- "He needs understanding."
- "He had a little too much to drink."
- "I should have had dinner ready for him on time."
- "I shouldn't have said anything about his mother."
- "Men will be men."
- "He promised me he wouldn't do it again."
- "He was jealous."
- "He can't control his temper."
- "He loves me."

BECKY'S DENIAL

Becky was a young unmarried woman with a three-year-old son. She met Sam and fell in love with him. Sam was good to her son; he took him places and provided a good father figure. Sam had shared some very personal memories of his childhood with her, memories of pain and abuse. He told her that her love erased his pain and gave him the love he never had. They got married.

After one year of marriage, she sought counseling. Sam's sexual practices were demanding and demeaning and he had also physically abused her son. However, they were receiving counseling and she felt the situation was under control. She sought counseling because she felt she was not complying with his sexual demands and was confused about why she couldn't comply. Perhaps the matter of her son was complicating things, but she didn't know how.

After talking and establishing a trusting bond, she admitted that Sam's sexual practices hurt her and made her feel ashamed and degraded. Once the denial of her pain was broken through, other issues emerged that she could begin to recognize. Becky had denied her feelings because she felt Sam needed her to heal his hurts. While in counseling, Becky was able to see her denial and explain why she clung to it. To admit that she was failing in her second relationship with a man, to lose a father figure for her son and to think that she could not meet her partner's sexual demands were gut issues she was avoiding at the expense of her well-being and her son's.

Denial is functional. It helps maintain the status quo. You can use it to cover or avoid solutions, to lie to yourself or to keep from leaving. You cannot use it to recover or to improve your life.

LACK OF SUPPORT

The response you receive when you ask for help strongly influences what happens next. Without support from friends, family and social services, women often stay trapped in abusive relationships. The following examples illustrate the powerful role support, or the absence of it, plays when trying to leave an abusive relationship.

JUNE: HER MOTHER SAID TO TRY HARDER

June told her mother that her husband was beating her and her mother's response was to "try harder." June stayed. Eventually, she was forced to flee from her husband, taking refuge one night in a friend's house. The next morning her husband appeared at the friend's door, telling her how much he loved and needed June. The friend let him in, and then urged June to return home because she hated to see him so hurt. The friend had not supported June, nor did she really understand the dynamics of abuse. June's feelings were virtually ignored. She felt she had no choice but to return to her husband.

June went to a marriage counselor with her husband. Before going, he warned her not to bring up anything about "family business," meaning the abuse. His drinking problem was brought out and addressed in counseling, but the abuse was never mentioned. And it never stopped. Although she left several times, she always went back.

A year or so later, she came for help and told her story. While she was at the shelter, her husband went to a detoxification center. June talked with his counselor, who asked her to go to the detoxification center to talk with him and her husband. We discussed the need to address the problem of her abuse as part of his treatment program. She went to the meeting, brought up the problem and the counselor talked about it. Feeling very hopeful, she thought the abuse would stop.

Confident that the counselor would be working with her husband on his abusive behavior, she began planning to go home. We talked about how abusive behavior takes time to change and depends on the man's motivations to change. We worked out a safety plan and she left.

One week later he was back living with her. In a telephone conversation she disclosed that his behavior had not really changed, but she did not know what else to do. We discussed separation for a designated time, but she thought that since she had talked to his counselor and her husband was trying, she could not desert him. Another complication was that he had moved back into the house and she could not get him out.

Expecting a magical turnaround in his behavior, she was disappointed in the help her husband had received. A few months later he was jailed for beating her.

JESSICA: "NEVER HAD IT SO GOOD"?

Jessica went to a psychologist because she was having problems with stress. Her health had deteriorated and she was having problems dealing with everyday events. The psychologist told her she was an abused woman.

She had been married for twenty-some years and never thought she was abused, but instead, thought that she herself was the problem. A long time ago she had told her mother how she felt about her husband and his treatment of her. Her mother's response was that she never had it so good and should be thankful he provided for her. Jessica never told another person about her relationship with her husband until she consulted the psychologist. Within a year after consulting him, she left and has never gone back. She is now in a loving relationship.

RHONDA: THEY SAID SHE CAUSED HER OWN ABUSE

Rhonda had been beaten by her husband for several years. A few years back, she and her husband had tried marital counseling. The subject of abuse came up and the counselor asked Rhonda what she did to cause her husband to abuse her! She carried that response with her for more than two years before she sought help from a women's center. She related that she didn't believe in her heart that she had caused the abuse, but she felt everyone else believed it, so she must accept the blame.

When an abused woman opens up and tells someone about the abuse she has gone through, she is taking a great risk. The response she receives can make a difference in the quality of her life from then on. A response of not wanting to talk about it implies that abuse is a taboo subject, distasteful, bad, ugly and something no one wants to hear about. Questioning the woman about what she did to cause or deserve the abuse tells the woman that she is to blame. Telling her to take it, try harder or ignore it confuses her even further and implies that she can control the abuse. These responses communicate a lack of support, furthering the isolation and despair she feels.

ISOLATION

Isolation is physical and emotional distance from others. There are many ways abused women are isolated. If an abused woman thinks that no other women are experiencing what she is experiencing, she feels isolated. She thinks she's the only one who lives this way.

If she thinks she caused the abuse, she feels alone in the sense that she believes she must be an awful person to have done this. "Surely," she thinks, "no one will want to have anything to do with this awful person." Even though she did not cause the abuse and is not an awful person, her believing so sets her apart from other people. She feels alone. It takes great courage to break this isolation.

JUDY: A PRISONER IN HER OWN HOME

Judy is an example of an isolated, abused woman. She lived in a small town and had two children. Her husband worked a split-shift job, which meant that one week he worked from 7 A.M. to 3 P.M. and the next week from 3 P.M. to 11 P.M. When he was not working, he was either sleeping or out drinking with the guys.

They had one vehicle and she was not allowed to use it unless she had his permission. If she needed to go to the store, she had to go with him. On rare occasions she was allowed to go out alone, but only under certain conditions. She had to be back when he designated or else she would be in trouble, which meant a beating. When she did return within her allotted time, she suffered a barrage of accusations about what men she saw, went to bed with, flirted with or teased. Eventually, she let him do all the shopping in order to avoid the ugly scene she knew she would have to face when she returned home.

Other than her occasional outings to shop, she was not allowed to go anywhere. If she went outside to chat with the neighbor and her husband found out, she would go through the jealousy and accusation scene again. This woman was physically isolated from everyone except her husband and children.

In order to escape she used the phone. She broke her isolation. She called the shelter's hotline number and talked with someone who expressed care and concern. Gradually she began to open up and tell her story, testing the listener as she progressed, wary of what the response might be to her story. She was also testing herself. How far could she go in revealing her personal circumstances? She was breaking through her isolation and establishing a personal support system. Eventually, she was able to find ways to get out and be with other people. What she learned from the telephone talks was how to get some of her needs met from more than one source.

ETHEL: EXTREME PHYSICAL AND EMOTIONAL ISOLATION

Ethel experienced a form of extreme physical and emotional isolation. She lived on a farm that was 20 miles from the nearest town and five miles from the nearest neighbor. The family had one truck, which the husband used to drive to work and to go out drinking. Ethel was in her late forties and had never learned to drive. Most of the telephone calls she made were toll calls, so extra charges were added to the bill and the phone number was listed for each call. She was allowed to call her sister and mother a certain number of times a month, but any other calls were challenged by her husband. She had to be prepared to give him a reason for each call she made.

Ethel was totally isolated from everyone. If her sister or mother had not come out to visit her and occasionally to take her places, she would never have left the house. Her sister called the shelter, asked if Ethel could come in and then took her there.

While at the shelter, Ethel learned about the dynamics of alcoholism and what she could and could not do about it. She also learned ways to get out of the house and break her isolation. For example, she loved to go to church and found a neighbor who would drive her to church every Sunday. She went back home, as she never had any intentions of leaving her husband; she just wanted to find out how she could make him change. Instead, she found ways to make changes in her own life, learning to handle more effectively her husband's drinking problems. She had broken her isolation, and although she chose not to leave, she was no longer as alone as she had been.

SOCIAL EXPECTATIONS

There are many expectations that society places on a woman. Some of these expectations can work against her leaving an abusive relationship. The marital contract is a good example of social expectations. Marriage is "for better or for worse." Does that mean that a wife must take abuse as the "worse" part of the marriage contract?

The belief that women "nourish" the family and keep it together is instilled in women at an early age. It is also instilled in men. He and she both expect her to keep the family together. If a woman leaves a man because he is abusing her, she is breaking up the family and must deal with this guilt. The fact that she couldn't take the abuse any more, and has the right to not be abused, is ignored by the abuser and many members of society.

What happens in the home is considered a private or family matter; society is not to impinge on a family's right of privacy. Of all the abused women we have known who have left their husbands, we do not recall a single husband who admitted his wife left because he abused her. Because she feels the degradation and humiliation of being abused, she is not about to advertise that she left as a result of abuse. The abused women we have known who have told people why they left received reactions ranging from disbelief, to ignorance that abuse was a problem, to pity. Society's acceptance of family violence as a way of life perpetuates the woman's fear of leaving or speaking out about her plight.

NO GUARANTEE OF SAFETY

There is no guarantee of safety if a woman decides to leave. If arrested, a husband is usually out on bail within 24 hours. If she gets a Protection From Abuse (PFA) order by the court, she still is the one who has to call the police and report that he is violating the PFA. What about in the meantime? She leaves and he comes after her; if he catches up with her, what protection does she have? Does she go out and get a gun to protect herself? Many women have, with the result that they may shoot him or he may shoot them.

SALLY: HE POINTED A GUN AT HER HEAD

Sally was married to a man who had repeatedly pointed a gun at her head. One night, while drunk, he got the gun out and threatened to shoot her and then himself. She stayed up all night with him trying to talk him out of it. She succeeded, and when he finally fell asleep, she left. She could not obtain a PFA because no one witnessed the incident and it would have been just her word against his.

She lived in a shelter for more than a month. Her friends told her he was hunting her and wanted to kill her. Her employer was also afraid for her. She didn't go to work during that month; she literally stayed in hiding.

When she returned to work, Sally and the manager devised a signal she could use to alert him that her husband was in the store. Her husband did come into the store and she used the signal. Her husband did not threaten her or make a scene, so he was not asked to leave. However, he was aware that Sally was surrounded by protective people. He asked Sally to meet him to talk, but she declined. She had resolved never again to be alone with this man.

The more an abused woman is isolated, depressed and full of fear, the greater the chance that she will be dominated by a "What's the use?" attitude. She believes there is no safe place to hide. To accept that someone or some place can protect you requires trust. Trust went out the window a lifetime ago for the abused woman.

LEARNED HELPLESSNESS

The idea that helplessness is learned was developed by Lenore E. Walker in her book *The Battered Woman* (1979). When a woman is repeatedly abused, she starts to believe that she can do nothing to stop it. The abuse continues in spite of her repeated attempts to stop it. The abused woman becomes convinced that she is permanently helpless. She becomes passive and depressed, feels powerless and believes that she must accept her abuse as a way of life. Once this faulty belief is adopted, it becomes difficult to refute. A vicious cycle is operating and she feels incapable of changing it and getting out.

Messages such as "Women are dependent on men"; "Women are the property of men"; and "Women are responsible for causing the abuse" feed into her belief system. The lack of support from the police, the law and the courts confirm her belief that she can do nothing to stop the abuse. Fear, dependency, denial and isolation contribute to the learned helplessness of an abused woman.

Once she believes she is helpless to stop her mate from abusing her, she gives up. She becomes anxious, never knowing when it will happen again. She becomes depressed by her feelings of futility and hopelessness. She does not try to act in ways that could be helpful to her. She loses her ability to think ahead and make plans for her safety. She believes no one can help her.

ERIN: "I ONLY WISH I HADN'T COME BACK"

Living with an alcoholic is one of the worst situations in a marriage. If the man you're involved with is violent and abusive to begin with, alcohol only makes it worse. It seems you can't win with an alcoholic. I tried to do everything possible not to upset my husband or cause him to drink. I know I don't cause him to drink or not drink, but that still doesn't stop me from trying everything possible.

I would try getting even by going places he didn't like or doing things to make him mad, but I was only hurting myself. I would try the opposite, doing everything I could to make him happy. I wouldn't go anywhere, thinking he would stay home with me. I was what I thought the perfect housewife should be. The house was always clean, supper was always on the table and the kids were well-behaved. I always tried to look my best. He was never happy, he always complained and he drank constantly. The kids and I were always miserable.

A couple of times I tried leaving him. I took nothing, hoping he would leave me and the kids alone. It was really hard to go. I always had a reason for leaving. I was either tired of the abuse or just fed up with his constant drinking. The kids would often say, "Mommy, why don't we leave Daddy?" and that's what made me realize things were not right. I thought it was worth it to get the kids out and live a normal life.

The first time I left, I went to my parents' house, which was a block away from our home. He came to the door and begged me to come back and promised he would stop drinking. I went back, but within a week the drinking started again. He would beat me up pretty bad when he got drunk.

The next time I left, I went to live with a friend. She had three kids, and with me and my two kids it was crowded. My husband, John, called the house all the time and would talk to my friend when he couldn't talk to me. She didn't know how to keep him away and neither did I.

The third time I left, I went to a shelter. We got some counseling and the kids and I talked about the problem and decided to get a place of our own.

Staying away from family, friends and home was harder than I thought it was going to be. I felt I couldn't be around my friends or family for fear John would show up or bother them. Being cut off from everyone was just too hard. The kids started to blame me because they missed their dad and blamed me for taking them away from their friends and relatives. The kids were eleven and six and knew what was going on at home. They were both excellent students and, like me, tried to do everything right, thinking they could make it better.

While we were away from home, they put me through hell. I needed to get a job to support us, but they wouldn't let me out of their sight because they were afraid I would leave them, too. They wanted to go home and hoped their dad had stopped drinking. Finally, I couldn't take anymore and went back to John with his promise to quit drinking. I thought I was doing the best thing for the kids, but soon John had broken his promises.

Now I realize that staying with John is the worst thing for the kids. Being raised in an alcoholic home, where we feel no love, will affect them for the rest of their lives. I feel there is no way out and I will have to spend the rest of my life with a man I can't stand. I thought I loved John and in some ways maybe I do. I realize I feel pity for him and don't want him to be alone. I would do anything or give up anything if John would just quit drinking. I'll probably have to spend the rest of my life waiting for things to get better.

I feel like a prisoner in my own home. He sees to it that I can't go anywhere or see anyone. My leaving didn't accomplish a thing. We did go to Al-Anon and AA for two weeks, but then he decided he could do it on his own and wouldn't let me go to Al-Anon.

I only wish I hadn't come back. It never gets better; it only gets worse. Now I can't tell my family or friends how bad it is because I will have to admit I was wrong to come back. The hardest thing to deal with is that I promised the kids I would not take them home to the same bad situation and to an alcoholic father.

I will always be afraid to love someone again. I tried to love John, but my love just made him more comfortable and able to drink more. I want to get the courage to leave him and never go back, but I don't think I can do it. I feel I am weak and can't do anything to help myself.

SHE LOVES HIM

Many abused women stay because they still love their men. Remember, the abuse may not always be a constant occurrence. These women live for the good times in between. As time passes and the abuse escalates, the good times are separated by longer intervals of pain and suffering. Yet, at the beginning of their relationships there were many fun and caring times. These good times are remembered with the hope that somehow the magic will return.

After an abusive episode, both parties feel bad, remorseful and sorry it ever happened. He promises never to do it again and gets her to promise to forgive and forget. They may go out and have fun, like on a first date, or make love to re-establish a bond between them. They both believe the abuse will never happen again. This stage does not last long; for some couples, not even a week. Inevitably, the battering resumes.

Lenore Walker (1979) describes the repeated cycle of abuse, which has three stages. The first stage begins with the tension-building phase, characterized by frustrations, lashing out by the male and little outbursts of abuse. The woman accepts his abusiveness and believes she can prevent his anger from escalating. The tension continues to build until it reaches a point of explosion.

The second stage is the explosion or acute abuse stage, distinguished by the male being out of control and enraged. This is the shortest of the three stages but is also the most lethal. Severe abuse and the most extreme forms of violence occur during this stage. Many women deny the seriousness of their injuries and abuse and are grateful the siege has ended.

Phase three manifests loving, kind and regretful behavior. The abuser says he's sorry and tries to make it up to her. He is convinced he can control himself and she believes him. This is the time she sees as the good time, when they are in love with each other and are trying to work things out. The only problem is that stage three doesn't last; the vicious cycle soon repeats itself.

SHE KEEPS HOPING HE'LL CHANGE

"I thought if I could just prove to him how much I loved him, he'd change" is a statement we often hear. Proving how much she loved him included taking his abuse. If he told her to drop her friends, she did. If he told her he was jealous of her male co-workers, she quit her job. If he told her she made him hit her, she agreed and tried to do better. It goes on and on. Abused women often cling to the notion that he'll change. After an episode, they talk. He says he's sorry and she's sure he'll change because he sees how hurt she is. Then there is another episode and more false hopes, until after a while there are no apologies, just silence. Still, she keeps hoping he'll change.

Abused women have begged authorities, counselors and family members to talk to the abuser and make him see how abusive he is in hopes he will change. It would be so much easier if only he'd stop his abuse and she wouldn't have to make all the changes. It doesn't work that way.

ELLEN: SHE THOUGHT HE COULD CHANGE

Drugs came into my life in 1980, when my husband started having recreational weekends with cocaine. The man next door was a dealer, so it was easy for my husband to get drugs. We had been married for ten years and I thought we didn't have any major marital problems.

My husband was a veteran of the Vietnam war and had always suffered bouts of depression and anxiety, but due to his past I always thought he was doing the best he could. I also thought he could change and would be able to do so with my help. He never abused me before he started on drugs.

However, I learned much later in counseling that I had been abused in other ways before he started taking drugs. At the time I didn't think it was abuse because he never physically laid a hand on me. I was a victim of his sexual abuse for years, but it never occurred to me that I was actually being abused. I also thought that if I went along with what he wanted, he'd finally be happy with me and change.

With the cocaine and alcohol his abuse increased, and within a year after he started using drugs, our marriage began to fall apart. The first time my husband attacked me happened after I had been out with my girlfriends. He had agreed to let me go out with them. The next morning he was very angry with me for being brought home by a male friend of ours. He came after me and choked me until I passed out. Afterwards he was scared and apologetic and I, too, was afraid.

I forgave him, although I knew we had a serious problem and I should get help. But I ignored it. From that point on I saw my husband do more drugs, get more depressed and turn on me. He was physically, mentally and sexually abusive toward me.

I could usually tell when he would lose control. There was a pattern to his madness. He would tell me it was okay to do something, then after I did it he would become furious with me. He would verbally attack me or yell and hit me. I would start to cry and he would say he was sorry and then want to make love to me. Making love seemed to reassure him that I still loved him. Even though I was disgusted, I would go along with it because I wanted him to get better and I thought this would help him.

My pattern in this madness was to do what he told me to do and after I did it, I would get in trouble for doing it. He would insist I go out with our friends, but he wouldn't go. When I came home, he would be furious and abuse me. Afterwards I was afraid of him and tried to please him so he wouldn't abuse me again. I was so ashamed I couldn't tell anyone. It was a horrible secret between the two of us.

I did talk to him about going for help but he refused. The more I begged him to get help, the more he attacked me.

I was putting on a pretty good front for the public, but inside I was dying. My self-esteem was nil and I felt like I was losing my sanity. I felt sub-human and very paranoid around him and other people. I was scared and depressed and felt like I was trapped in a corner with no way out. I had lost weight and did not look good. I tried to hide the bruises from the kids and other people because I was so embarrassed and so ashamed. I was having diarrhea and vomiting on a regular basis.

I felt responsible for him and for keeping the family together. My belief was that the woman is the heart of the family and she is the one to keep the family together: I am not as important as my husband and children. I would forget about myself and take care of them. I also had this faith in my husband that he could lick this problem but he needed my help to do so. I felt I had failed and had let things get to this point. The only thing that kept me going was my children, although they were nervous and scared by all of the turmoil.

The point that made me seek help was when he started verbally attacking the girls and threatening suicide. I took my husband to the VA hospital and told them he needed help. My husband voluntarily entered the hospital. I talked to his doctor and told him what had been happening at home. I told my husband and the doctor I wanted a divorce because I couldn't take it anymore.

After my husband was there for about a week, the doctor called me and told me he needed to come home and see his family because he missed us so much. The doctor felt this visit would help my husband. The doctor also agreed with me that my husband was an abusive man and that I should be afraid of him. How could he send my husband home when he knew we were afraid of him? My husband discharged himself from the hospital and came home. He made more threats of suicide and tried to jump in front of a truck on the highway. I called the hospital but they could not take him because there were no self-inflicted wounds on him and he would not commit himself.

I was a mess. I couldn't take his threats and didn't know where to turn for help. I wanted someone to stop my husband, to make him better, to make him change.

I went to a women's center for help. I wanted to learn how to deal with my children. I learned some ways to talk to my children and sat down with them and had an honest talk. An honest talk meant I had to drop the front and admit what was happening. We talked about the abuse, the drug problems, wanting a divorce and not knowing what to do next.

I was concerned that they know their father had always and still loved them, but the drugs made him do awful things. This was the beginning of our talking with each other and sharing our feelings. Some of their feelings toward me have been angry and hurtful and it has not been easy for me to deal with them.

Another thing I learned in counseling is to deal with myself. I went for help for my children, but I received it mainly for myself. I am important, my feelings matter and I have to take care of myself before I can take care of anyone else. I learned how to deal with my husband and stand up for myself. I started to get my self-esteem back and realized I was not responsible for my husband's actions. It was not my fault that he was abusive.

As I continued to get counseling, I could sense a change in me for the better. This was not an easy or quick process for me. It took me over a year to work this out. Now I am living with my children on my own. I have a job and must scrape by to make it. But I can proudly say I am happy and in control of my life. My husband still shows up now and again and there are problems, but I am safe and he can't hurt me anymore.

Actual cases reveal that few abused women stay in an abusive relationship for any single reason described in this chapter. Several motives usually combine to form a complex pattern. Clearly understanding why she stays prepares an abused woman to gain insight into what she needs, her alternatives and the resources she will need to support her decisions.

Insight alone will not solve the problems. How she feels about her life and her ability to work through these feelings become critical factors in seeking help.

Depression, fear and lack of trust are three powerful feelings that result from abuse. Depression is a way to numb other feelings, especially anger, and is a way to get through life even if it means just going through the motions. Fear is a devastating feeling that gives rise to helplessness because she cannot escape. The belief that her survival depends on appeasing her abuser arises from her fear.

Lack of trust in herself and others accompanies abuse. If you love and trust someone who violates that trust by hurting you, you will think that this can happen in all relationships. You become reluctant to trust anyone and may antagonize or push away those who could help you.

Finally, help will not occur without change. If nothing is done, nothing will happen. Regardless of the number or kinds of reasons for staying, they all have one thing in common: they keep the victim in the abusive relationship. It takes action to break the abuse cycle. Hoping that he will change will only change the victim while hope slips away.

AFTERTHOUGHTS

The hardest thing to believe when you are young is that people will fight to stay in a rut, but not to get out of it.

—Ellen Glasgow

Martyrdom does not end something, it is only a beginning.

—Indira Gandhi

Advice is what we ask for when we already know the answer but wish we didn't.

—Erica Jong

The only time a woman really succeeds in changing a man is when he's a baby.

—Natalie Wood

Many women do not recognize themselves as discriminated against; no better proof could be found of the totality of their conditioning.

—Kate Millett

V

The Effects of Too Much Drinking on the Family

*Whoever inquires about our childhood wants to know
something about our soul.*

—Alice Walker

If drinking is causing problems in personal relationships, health or self-care and the individual continues to drink, then that person has a drinking problem. This drinking problem is called alcoholism. Like spouse abuse, it cannot be denied away. It continues to get worse, the same as abusive behavior. That is why it is called a progressive disease.

While alcoholism progresses, it affects everyone around it. You are affected by his alcoholism, and if you have children, so are they. Families can respond in many ways to alcoholism. However, the results are usually the same: feelings of shame, guilt, confusion, depression, denial, anger and despair. Although most alcoholics will tell you that their drinking does not affect anyone but them, there are approximately 40 million non-alcoholic spouses and children of alcoholics in this country who will tell you otherwise! You and your family are affected, and you and your family are responding to the drinking whether you want to admit it or not. Usually, he is addicted to alcohol and everyone in the family is addicted to him (co-dependency). Just as with abuse, you and your family must react to a condition that is seldom understood, usually denied, but always emotionally painful.

Responses to alcoholism in the family can be divided into four phases. These are the reactive, active, alternative and family unity phases. These different periods are distinguished by several characteristics that dominate each particular phase. Not all alcoholic families experience these conditions similarly, nor are they universally progressive; not all families will progress from one phase to the next. Many families, unfortunately, remain in the first phase and never reach the fourth state of sobriety and family growth.

PHASE I—THE REACTIVE PHASE

In the reactive phase, nonalcoholic family members mainly react to the alcoholic's behavior. Family members behave cautiously to avoid further complicating the existing problems of alcoholism. However, by being reactive, they are constantly adapting their behavior in order to minimize or survive an unhealthy situation. Much of this adaptation will not only have detrimental effects on those who are adapting, but will also indirectly allow and support the continuing alcoholism. During the reactive phase, three typical family characteristics emerge: family denial, coping strategies and social disengagement.

FAMILY DENIAL

It is ironic that family members deny a drinking problem in their family because this is exactly what the alcoholic does, too. We know that, for the alcoholic, denial is functional: it allows the alcoholic to continue drinking. As long as the alcoholic denies the problem, there is no reason to seek a solution. Non-alcoholic family members also deny, but their denial is completely dysfunctional. It does them no good whatsoever. Everyone in the family denies that something is wrong, yet no one feels right. Family denial of alcoholism occurs in at three least forms: as systemic denial, as protection against exposure and as the primary patient philosophy.

Systemic Denial

Systemic denial means that the entire system denies the existence of a problem. A family is analogous to a system, which is a pattern of interrelationships. Within the family system, denial usually occurs when family members do not want to admit that one of them is an alcoholic, or because they perceive alcoholism as a negative reflection upon themselves.

This is particularly true for nonalcoholic wives. In American society, if the husband has a drinking problem, there is often a connotation that the wife is partly responsible. Statements such as "She drove him to drink!" are typical. Even though statements like this are not factually correct, the woman may perceive them as true and somehow accept responsiblity for his alcoholism. Therefore, as long as she denies that her husband has a drinking problem, she can deny that she had anything to do with causing the problem. Does this pattern sound similar to abuse? It sure does to us!

Another form of systemic denial occurs at the societal level. The family itself is also part of a larger system, the community or society in which it resides. Our society does not readily admit to alcohol problems. Although we accept alcoholism as a disease (medically, but not legally), there still are many who attach a moral stigma or deviant status to alcoholism. It is unreasonable to blame a family for covering up a condition that is not fully understood by society.

Protection Against Exposure

A second form of family denial is protection against exposure. Protection means sheltering oneself or another by not talking about the problem. Exposure means not only experiencing the problem, but recognizing it, discussing it and overcoming its effects. In the alcoholic home, the nonalcoholic spouse will often try to protect the children from exposure.

A universal form of protection is to treat the alcohol problem as if it did not exist. While this is impossible in a home where both parents are alcoholics, it is common for a nonalcoholic parent to say, "I have to cover up because I want to protect my children." Usually this means that alcohol abuse is never discussed, especially with the children. This would be fine if protection were the problem, but trying to protect children from a reality to which they are continuously exposed is a form of denial. In essence, the exposure is denied, any effects from the exposure are denied and more important, the need for help is denied.

To assume that children in an alcoholic home do not know and feel the effects of alcoholism is naive. They know. They may not understand, but they know. Living in an alcoholic home is not a "spectator sport." Everyone is involved to one degree or another, including the passive participants.

Primary Patient Philosophy

The third form of denial is the "primary patient philosophy." In the past, when alcoholism existed in a family, it was assumed that the alcoholic was the primary concern. The alcoholic needed to be helped first. Most alcoholics do not quit drinking, however, and while we are waiting for their sobriety, families fall apart, marriages collapse, abuse continues and children grow up and leave home. As long as we consider the alcoholic the primary concern, we deny intervention for the non-alcoholic family members.

The welfare of nonalcoholic family members should be considered the priority, not the alcoholic. Isn't it about time you and your family came first? This is not to say you should ignore the alcoholic, but rather to insure that you do not ignore the effects of alcoholism on your family while he's still drinking.

COPING STRATEGIES

Adaptation is the key to surviving in an alcoholic home. You learn to adapt your behavior to minimize the effects of alcoholism. Coping strategies are developed within the alcoholic home even when the family denies the existence of alcoholism. Denial within the home is no longer as strong, perhaps, but it is maintained outside of the household. For this reason, coping strategies are "home remedies." They are efforts by nonalcoholic families to survive a situation while denying its existence to others. These strategies are severely limited and seldom work. Coping strategies can be either verbal or behavioral. At best they provide a brief, but anxious, respite.

Verbal Coping Strategies

Verbal strategies are efforts by nonalcoholic family members to communicate effectively with the alcoholic about alcoholism, efforts which are usually interpreted by the alcoholic as "nagging" or persecution. The nonalcoholic resorts to morality lectures, pleas for self-respect, threats, promises and statements such as "How could you do this to us?" Unfortunately, most verbal strategies do little to motivate the alcoholic, but do a lot to increase everyone's anxiety.

Behavioral Coping Strategies

The second type of coping strategy is behavioral. The behavioral strategies are behaviors that nonalcoholic families knowingly or unknowingly adopt to cope with their predicament. Typical behavior strategies are hiding alcohol, refusing to buy alcohol, marking bottles, avoiding the alcoholic or other family members, staying away from home and isolating oneself. Many families deny that they have developed coping strategies, but it is difficult to deny their unusual behavior. In a home where drinking is permitted and is within normal acceptable limits, family members do not engage in this unusual behavior. Where drinking is abnormal, abnormal nonalcoholic behaviors exist. As a result of these coping strategies, nonalcoholic family members become socially disengaged from friends, family, community and themselves.

As stated earlier, many nonalcoholic family members deny or are unaware of their use of coping strategies. The following questionnaire was developed for nonalcoholic family members, to help overcome their denial of the effects of alcoholism in their lives. Note that most of these questions pertain to the behavior of nonalcoholic family members.

Family members should answer the following questions honestly:

1. Do you lose sleep because of a problem drinker?
2. Do most of your thoughts revolve around the problem drinker or problems that arise because of him or her?
3. Do you exact promises about the drinking that are not kept?
4. Do you make threats or decisions and not follow through on them?
5. Has your attitude changed toward this problem drinker (alternating between love and hate)?
6. Do you mark, hide, dilute and/or empty bottles of liquor or medication?
7. Do you think that everything would be okay if only the problem drinker would stop or control the drinking?
8. Do you feel alone, fearful, anxious, angry and frustrated most of the time? Are you beginning to feel dislike for yourself and to wonder about your sanity?
9. Do you find your moods fluctuating wildly as a direct result of the problem drinker's moods and actions?
10. Do you feel responsible and guilty about the drinking problem?
11. Do you try to conceal, deny or protect the problem drinker?

12. Have you withdrawn from outside activities and friends because of embarrassment and shame over the drinking problem?

13. Have you taken over many chores and duties that you would normally expect the problem drinker to assume or that were formerly his or hers?

14. Do you feel forced to try to exert tight control over the family expenditures with less and less success, and are financial problems increasing?

15. Do you feel the need to justify your actions and attitudes and, at the same time, feel somewhat smug and self-righteous compared with the drinker?

16. If there are children in the house, do they often take sides with either the problem drinker or the spouse?

17. Are the children showing signs of emotional stress, such as withdrawing, having trouble with authority figures, rebelling or acting out sexually?

18. Have you noticed physical symptoms in yourself, such as nausea, a "knot" in the stomach, ulcers, shakiness, sweating palms or bitten fingernails?

19. Do you feel utterly defeated—that nothing you say or do will move the problem drinker? Do you believe that he or she can't get better?

20. Where this applies, is your sexual relationship with a problem drinker affected by feelings of revulsion; do you "use" sex to manipulate or refuse sex to punish him or her?

Here are some additional questions specifically for children of alcoholics, to help them assess their feelings about parental alcoholism (Brooks, 1981):

1. Do you worry about your mom's or dad's drinking?

2. Do you sometimes feel that you are the reason your parent drinks so much?

3. Are you ashamed to have your friends come to your house, and are you finding more and more excuses to stay away from home?
4. Do you sometimes feel that you hate your parents when they are drinking and then feel guilty for hating them?
5. Have you been watching how much your parents drink?
6. Do you try to make your parents happy so they won't get upset and drink more?
7. Do you feel you can't talk about the drinking in your home—or even how you feel inside?
8. Do you sometimes drink or take drugs to forget about things at home?
9. Do you feel that if your parents really loved you, they wouldn't drink so much?
10. Do you sometimes wish you had never been born?
11. Do you want to start feeling better?

SOCIAL DISENGAGEMENT

Social disengagement is the withdrawing of family members from interaction with others. The family literally denies itself the support structure that it needs. This withdrawal is exacerbated because the family feels that it must protect itself, has been embarrassed or fears future encounters with others where the alcoholic is present. The family becomes isolated, and feels that there is a lack of available alternatives. The home becomes a "habit cage."

Families of alcoholics need not become isolated if they do not choose to be. Most rarely feel that they have a choice, however; they see their only response as withdrawal. This social disengagement can occur as either physical or emotional withdrawal.

Physical Disengagement

Physical disengagement occurs when the family stops receiving and giving invitations for social interaction. The family is pulled back from physical contact with others. Children, for example, no longer invite their friends to their homes. Nonalcoholic spouses hide invitations to functions involving alcohol to avoid any confrontations or embarrassment. Fewer people stop by to visit because of the unpleasantness or tension from a previous visit. The family becomes significantly separated as a unit from others. This physical isolation can lead to emotional disengagement.

Emotional Disengagement

Emotional disengagement is a decline in positive emotional relationships. In the alcoholic home this decline is combined with an increase in negative emotions. The longer the alcoholism continues and the more the family withdraws, the greater the probability that negative emotions such as tension, anxiety, despair and powerlessness will emerge. One method of handling these negative emotions is to attempt to become "nonfeeling," to deny and minimize negative feelings to prevent further pain. Thus avoidance becomes the norm for handling negative emotions, even though avoidance also leads to the denial of benefits from positive relationships, which could be offsetting factors for the negative ones. The goals of positive relationships are sacrificed for the "comfortableness" of isolation within the family.

Of all the problems encountered by nonalcoholic family members, emotional isolation may be the greatest. It not only affects life within the family, but also outside the family. Healthy relationships are denied or postponed to survive an unhealthy situation. Most non-alcoholic family members never assess the negative impact of this approach; they do what they believe makes the most sense at the time. The real impact may be found outside the family or for children in their adult lives. This is particularly true when considering that the children of alcoholics are disproportionately represented in juvenile courts, family courts, spouse and child abuse cases, divorces and within populations plagued with psychological or emotional problems as adults.

Unfortunately, many families of alcoholics do not go beyond the reactive phase. They deny that the problem drinker is alcoholic, they helplessly hope for recovery or they passively participate in the alcoholism syndrome. This stagnation at the reactive phase commonly leads to the following effects on the alcoholic, the nonalcoholic spouse and the children.

During the reactive phase the alcoholic:
- Denies the alcohol problem; blames others; forgets and tells stories to defend and protest against humiliation, attack and criticism from others in the family
- Spends money for day-to-day needs on alcohol
- Becomes unpredictable and impulsive in behavior
- Resorts to verbal and physical abuse in place of honest open talk
- Loses the trust of family, relatives and friends
- Experiences a diminishing sexual drive
- Has feelings of despair and hopelessness
- Thinks about suicide and possibly makes an attempt

The spouse:
- Often tries to hide and deny the existing problem of the alcoholic
- Takes on the responsibilities of the other person, carrying the load of two and perpetrating the spouse dependence
- Takes a job to get away from the problem and/or maintain financial security
- Finds it difficult to be open and honest because of resentment, anger and hurt feelings
- Avoids sexual contact
- May over-protect the children, neglect them and/or use them for emotional support
- Shows gradual social withdrawal and isolation
- May lose feelings of self-respect and self-worth
- May use alcohol or prescription drugs in an effort to cope

The children:
- May be victims of birth defects

- May be torn between parents: being loyal to one, they arouse and feel the anger of the other
- May be deprived of emotional and physical support
- Avoid peer activities, especially in the home, out of fear and shame
- Learn destructive and negative ways of dealing with problems and getting attention
- Lack trust in anyone
- May lose sight of values, standards and goals because of the absence of consistent, strong parenting
- Suffer a dimishing sense of self-worth as a significant member of the family

PHASE II—THE ACTIVE PHASE

The main differences between the active and reactive phases are the responses of the nonalcoholic family members, even though the alcoholic is still drinking. Rather than being passive to the effects on themselves from alcoholism, they begin to take an active interest in themselves. No longer do they perceive themselves as totally under the alcoholic's control, and they attempt to gain some control over their own lives. In this manner the family begins to "de-center" itself from alcoholism. In addition, family denial of alcoholism is not as strong. A major step into the active phase is the overcoming of denial by family members. They begin to realize that the problem cannot be denied away. Likewise, they are willing to abandon their anonymity in exchange for help and for a viable alternative to the way they have been living. The two predominant characteristics of the active phase are awareness of the problems and striving to be normal.

AWARENESS

During the active phase, family members develop a growing awareness about alcoholism, their family and themselves. Some of the awarenesses that develop are:

- They are not responsible for causing the alcoholism
- They do not have to live like this; alternatives are available
- They recognize the need for help
- They realize that help is available
- They are not alone and do not have to be alone

Much of this active time for nonalcoholic family members is spent becoming involved in their own recovery. They begin to involve themselves in various educational, counseling and self-help groups. During this time they may begin to realize that they, too, are important, and that even the failure of the alcoholic to stop drinking should not necessarily prevent them from getting help. During the reactive phase they may have assumed that nothing could be done until the alcoholic received help. In the active phase they realize that waiting may be futile, denies their own needs and only perpetuates and reinforces the impact of alcoholism on their lives.

BEING NORMAL

During this period the nonalcoholic family members, particularly the nonalcoholic spouse, attempt to stabilize the alcoholic home. Despite active alcoholism (alcoholism is considered active as long as the alcoholic is still drinking), they decide to "get on with" normal family activities as much as possible. Even though it is desirable for the alcoholic to quit drinking and become a part of the normalizing process, sobriety is not a prerequisite. It's true that active alcoholism will impede the process, but what is actually happening during the normal stage is an open and honest attempt to make the best of a negative situation inside and outside the home in order to overcome the negative impacts of alcoholism. This is particularly true if the abused woman decides to stay in the relationship. The idea that families can begin their recovery process and become involved in normal activities that they once avoided begins to take hold.

These activities may include children becoming involved in school and group activities, joining self-help groups, encouraging family conversations and sharing feelings. These endeavors do not necessarily pertain to alcoholism and recovery, which is significant in itself. Perhaps more important is that they do pertain to the normal activities of children who are not in alcoholic homes. These "other" activities have their benefits not only in the activities themselves, but also in the separation from alcoholism. These can serve as positive outside factors offsetting a negative home environment, as well as contribute to building better family interaction patterns. Again, paramount to this phase is overcoming denial, risking the loss of anonymity and once again taking an active interest in their lives by the nonalcoholic family members. These steps begin with awareness of the desire to feel normal.

PHASE III—THE ALTERNATIVE PHASE

The alternative phase begins when all else has failed. The family now faces the painful question of whether or not separation is the only viable alternative to survive alcoholism. It is not necessary that a family progress through both of the two previous phases. Some families will go directly from the reactive phase into the alternative phase, while others will attempt the active phase before making the decision to separate. The characteristics of the alternative phase are polarization, separation, change and family reorganization.

POLARIZATION

Prior to separation, many alcoholic families go through a process of polarization: family members begin to withdraw from each other and are often forced to "choose sides." Parents may begin to make threats to each other or inform the children that they are considering a legal separation or divorce. Unfortunately, alcoholism contributes to approximately 40 percent of family court cases, and many children of alcoholics experience the additional difficulty of being not only children of alcoholics, but children of divorce as well. Polarization may also lead to a separation. In many cases this time of decision is long and painful, and in some cases may be more traumatic than the actual separation. For children it is a time of impending change and is often accompanied by feelings of confusion, torn loyalties, fear, resentment, anger and increased isolation.

SEPARATION

For some families the only viable alternative left will be family separation. For others, the separation will only compound existing problems, and still others will only exchange one set of problems for a new set of problems. In short, for some life will get better, for others it will be about the same, and for still others it will get worse. For many children, separation will mean life without daily contact with the alcoholic. Even within the same family this change may be greeted with different feelings. For younger children the loss of the parental role is of more concern than the loss of the alcoholic parent, but for older children it may be the opposite. They may perceive that although they are losing the parental role, it was really already lost anyway. Much of their reaction will depend upon how the individual family members perceive this change in their lives.

CHANGE

There is a belief that change itself is always traumatic. This is incorrect. To assess the likely impact of change you must know both its rate and direction. If the rate of change is too rapid, it can be upsetting because of our inability to adjust quickly enough. On the other hand, change that lingers on and on without closure can produce intense anxiety.

Separation can be painful, but the way it happens can hurt, too. In some alcoholic families the process of polarization may have been a long and tedious affair, whereas in other families polarization occurred very rapidly and the decision to separate was made in haste. In some instances, however, it may be that the family members knew that it was time for a much-needed change and that the right time had arrived.

The direction of change becomes critical for each family member because personal needs and levels of understanding differ. Individual family members interpret impending change as being to their advantage or disadvantage. Children who think they will be worse off after separation view the change as undesirable and oppose it. On the other hand, if children foresee that their lives will improve, then the change is less problematic. Life without the alcoholic is perceived as better than life with the alcoholic. In reality, for some members of the alcoholic family this will be true and for others it will not. Much depends upon how the new family grows and is reorganized.

FAMILY REORGANIZATION

For alcoholic families that have chosen the alternative phase, several things can occur during reorganization. The family may begin to pull together and grow. In these families, members may begin to seek help for themselves or become further involved in their own recovery process. Family members will begin to feel good about themselves and establish healthy relationships within and outside their family.

For other families, reorganization will involve new and added roles. The custodial spouse now faces the single-parent challenge. Even though alcoholic parents are often absent, at times they do help in parenting. Children may have to shoulder added responsibilities. All the family members' new roles can, however, be impeded by old feelings such as resentment, anger, guilt, abandonment, failure and doubt that accompany being the child or the spouse of an alcoholic. These destructive feelings can be coupled with the old habit of continuously talking about the alcoholic, blaming problems on alcoholism or holding the alcoholic solely responsible for the problems in their lives.

Reorganization can be complicated further when separated alcoholic parents visit the family, particularly if they are still drinking. The alcoholic may use the children to "get at" the non-alcoholic spouse. The children may become pawns in a contest between spouses, especially if the alcoholic seeks the children's support for a reconciliation.

Even the alcoholic's attempts at reconciliation may receive mixed reactions within the same family. Younger children may favor the idea more than older children because they probably have not been exposed to the alcoholism for as long a time. One of the main problems of re-organization will be the tendency to fall back into many of the patterns of the reactive phase. A family will need support during the alternative phase if the alternatives are to become solutions.

PHASE IV—FAMILY UNITY PHASE

Many alcoholic families never reach the family unity phase because of continuing alcoholism. There are no distinct progressive patterns leading to the unity phase. Some families will proceed directly from phase one to phase four; others will go through the first two phases and then to four; and still others may go through all the phases on their way to family unity. When they arrive, however, the family will face at least three concerns that are characteristic of this phase: sobriety, the dry drunk and family growth.

SOBRIETY

Central to the family unity phase is the sobriety of the alcoholic. But sobriety alone may not be enough. Accepting the sober alcoholic back into the mainstream of the family is not always easy and certainly not automatic. Sobriety does not guarantee family growth; it only makes it possible. Just as the family does not cause alcoholism, sobriety does not immediately "cause" a healthy family.

The early stages of sobriety may contain some pitfalls. For example, the family probably has waited a long time for sobriety and now expects to enter "paradise." In many alcoholic families, the longer the alcoholism continues, the higher the probability that all family problems will be blamed on the bottle. Therefore, the family expects other problems to end when the drinking ends. But difficulties continue to exist, as they do in all families. Difficulties that were formerly believed to stem from alcoholism surface as ordinary family disagreements. In the past these problems may have been denied, as was the alcoholism, but now new ways of dealing with normal family problems will be needed.

Some families have heard promises of sobriety before and adopt a "wait and see" attitude before committing themselves to the family recovery process. Other families, however, will be more active and supportive of the newfound sobriety and will eagerly anticipate the normal family behaviors that have been missing.

THE DRY DRUNK

For families unable to join in the recovery process, much of their lives will remain the same. Even though the alcoholic has achieved sobriety, no other changes in the family are taking place. The breakdown in family communications continues to take its toll on the emotions of family members. This will be particularly true in an abusive situation. Unless the family is able to adapt to the sober alcoholic and themselves, and can become a unit and grow, the family may find itself on a "dry drunk."

In such cases, tension, anxiety and conflict persist because other problems have not been resolved. The family needs to understand that throughout the drinking days family relationships were never sufficiently established or were deteriorating. Some children in the "dry drunk" situation are unable to remember anything but the drinking behavior of one or both parents. Although the recovering alcoholic may actually be trying to parent properly, this is a new or strange behavior. It may not be entirely trusted within the family when the drinking stops. The family must be incorporated in a new adaptive process. To ignore the role of the family in helping recovering alcoholics maintain sobriety is to ignore the emotional impact that alcoholism has had on the family.

FAMILY GROWTH

If the abuse stops and the family members become emotionally reintegrated, there is potential for growth with or without the sober alcoholic. This family growth will mean that the family neither dwells on nor hides the past, but has learned from it. The growing family is one that goes beyond the past. It continues to change and improve, moving toward the goal of healthy family relationships. It is a family that is overcoming the negative influences of alcoholism and is discovering or rediscovering family unity.

If any of the preceding patterns sound familiar to you—if you have been living this way—you are probably in an alcoholic relationship. By combining the topics of spouse abuse and alcohol abuse we are not trying to paint the darkest possible picture. What we are trying to do is to help as many victims as possible see the situation for what it is and then make the necessary changes to improve their lives. Alcoholism is involved in many abusive relationships. And, as we stated earlier, there is no such thing as a non-abusive alcoholic relationship.

AFTERTHOUGHTS

Youth is, after all, just a moment, but it is the moment, the spark that you always carry in your heart.

—Raisa M. Gorbachev

What is buried in the past of one generation falls to the next to claim.

—Susan Griffin

There are many ways to be starved.

—Paxa Lourde

You must do the thing you think you cannot do.

—Eleanor Roosevelt

In the culture of domination, we are possessed without knowing it and without knowing techniques to free ourselves.

—Starhawk

VI

THE FALLEN ANGEL SYNDROME: WOMEN AND ALCOHOL

———————— ❧ ————————

It is very hard for me to think of my alcoholism as a failure because to me it was and is a disease.

—Ann Richards
Former Governor of Texas

We realize that most abused women are not alcoholic, but we also realize that there are so many alcoholic women who are also abused that it would be a serious omission not to include a discussion of their unique dilemma in this book.

The woman who has a drinking problem always has more than one problem; not only does she confront the alcoholism, but she must also handle the increased stigma that is often attached to the female alcoholic. This increased stigma, which attests that it is somehow less acceptable and more detrimental for a woman to have a drinking problem than for a man, is known as the "fallen angel" syndrome.

In most women's alcoholism treatment programs we discover that the female alcoholism client often abuses other drugs, is more likely to have experienced several life crises and is more likely to have been abused than the nonalcoholic client. Her denial is likely to be stronger than a man's because of these complications and the impact of the fallen angel syndrome.

These considerations lead to unique difficulties for the female alcoholic. She is widely misunderstood and misdiagnosed, suffers greater denial than the male alcoholic and is isolated. These facts combine to make the alcoholic woman a likely target for physical and emotional abuse. The female alcoholic's special characteristics and burdens contribute not only to her abuse, but also to the decreased likelihood of her seeking help.

There are four links in the chain that binds so many alcoholic women to abuse. First, many men have a very low tolerance level for alcoholism in women. They don't know how to handle it and become abusive. Second, most women cannot defend themselves against abuse when sober, let alone when intoxicated. Third, a woman's own guilt and remorse about her drinking lowers her self-esteem. When abused, she may rationalize the abuse because of her low opinion of herself. Fourth, like most alcoholics, she will deny that she has a drinking problem. If she seeks help for the abuse, she fears that her drinking will be exposed. So she does not seek help for either problem.

Drinking problems and abuse have another connection for women. The development of drinking problems for many women is related to a life crisis. They often begin to drink alcoholically because of something negative in their lives. Being abused or being in a troubled relationship are about as negative as you can get.

Later in this chapter we will explore other aspects of women and alcohol abuse. However, the first concern of all alcohol abuse begins and ends with denial. It is the key to discovery and to recovery. The following questionnaire was developed especially for women to assess their drinking practices.

1. Do you try to get someone to buy liquor for you because you are ashamed to buy it yourself?
2. Do you buy liquor at different places so no one will know how much you purchase?
3. Do you hide the empties and dispose of them secretly?
4. Do you plan in advance to "reward" yourself with a little drinking bout after you've worked hard in the house?
5. Are you often permissive with your children because you feel guilty about the way you behaved when you were drinking?
6. Do you have "blackouts," periods about which you remember nothing?
7. Do you phone the hostess of a party the next day and ask if you hurt anyone's feelings or made a fool of yourself?
8. Do you find cigarette holes in your clothes or the furniture and can't remember when it happened?
9. Do you take an extra drink or two before leaving for a party when you know liquor will be served there?
10. Do you often wonder if anyone knows how much you drink?
11. Do you feel wittier or more charming when you are drinking?
12. Do you feel panicky when faced with nondrinking days, such as a visit to out-of-town relatives?
13. Do you invent social occasions for drinking, such as inviting friends for lunch, cocktails or dinner?
14. When others are present, do you avoid reading articles or seeing movies or TV shows about women alcoholics, but read and watch when no one is around?
15. Do you ever carry liquor in your purse?
16. Do you become defensive when someone mentions your drinking?
17. Do you become irritated when unexpected guests reduce your liquor supply?
18. Do you drink when under pressure or after an argument?

19. Do you try to cover up when you can't remember promises and feel ashamed when you misplace or lose things?

20. Do you drive even though you've been drinking, but feel certain you are in complete control of yourself?

If you truthfully answered "yes" to half or more of these, go for help.

DONNA: VIOLENCE, PAINKILLERS AND ALCOHOL

My name is Donna. I am the mother of four children who are living with their father at this time. Right now I'm trying to better myself so that some day in the near future my children can come and live with me again.

I've had a rough life from childhood through adulthood, but after going through almost a year of counseling and going to a drug and alcohol rehabilitation center in August of 1987, I've learned that nobody is really to blame for the way my life turned out. It just happened, and I'm the only one who can change it.

When I was a child, I was the victim of child abuse. I was abused physically and verbally by my mother and sexually abused by my father. My counselor is working with me right now on the sexual abuse because I've blocked most of it from my mind. It hurts to remember some things, but it's a relief to have the blame taken off my shoulders.

To escape from my parents I left on my 18th birthday to marry the guy I thought was Prince Charming. Well, it ended up he was a drug dealer, a user and very abusive to me. He got me hooked on drugs, which made it harder for me to leave him as the years went by. He made me feel that without him I couldn't take care of the children or myself.

When I was 26, I started to get migraine headaches. The doctors started me on painkillers, which I got hooked on. One day in January of 1986 my husband was beating me up real bad and I saw two of my children standing at the glass doors, looking at me with tears running down their faces. I remember thinking, "My children are not going to go through this anymore." The next day I gathered the children and went to a women's center for protection.

It was not easy to be on my own with the children. I had to start from scratch to begin a whole new life that included no drugs. I was doing good for the first six months, staying clean, but then I started school full-time and the migraines started again. I went back on the painkillers. I ended up quitting school. When I couldn't get the painkillers, I was drinking alcohol.

During this time I filed for divorce and my husband tried everything to get me to come back. He threatened to take the children away from me and to contest the divorce. In January of 1987 I took too many painkillers and ended up in the hospital. But I didn't take them on purpose.

Now my husband thought, "Boy, do I have her right where I want her." He tried really hard to talk me into going back, but I knew it wouldn't work out. He came and forcibly took the children from me in June of 1987. It was then I realized I had a problem and needed help. I entered a treatment center. Between rehabilitation, counseling and meetings, I am finally putting my life together.

My husband is still using the children to try to get me back, but it won't work. I know I have to take control of my own life without drugs and alcohol because they don't solve my problems; they only make them worse. I know it's best that the children are not with me right now so I have time to work on myself. Someday I hope to get my children back and I won't stop fighting until they are with me.

OBSTACLES TO TREATMENT

An abused woman is at double risk if she has an alcohol problem. She is not in control of her life as a result of the alcohol and she is unable to defend herself from abuse. This gives rise to a vicious cycle in which she not only drinks and feels the guilt, remorse and shame from losing control, but also feels guilt, remorse and shame from being abused. She drinks to eliminate the symptoms of anxiety, stress and low self-confidence, and also to deaden the pain of abuse. Eventually, she can become addicted.

Many abused women have told us they originally tried drinking as a way of coping with being abused. Some tried it to keep up with their mates in response to the "If you can't lick them, join them" idea.

One woman, Darla, told us she began drinking with her partner in order not to be left out. Since drinking was his way of relaxing after work, she joined him in hopes of being able to be close. It didn't work out; they still had fights and he still beat her. The closeness she hoped to achieve did not develop. Instead, she put herself at a greater risk of abuse.

A woman may start drinking to help a mate. She may reason that if she drinks with him, she can somehow control how much he drinks. The catch is that she may become addicted and he may or may not. If both become addicted, their relationship develops deeper trouble.

If she is addicted and he stops drinking, she will fear losing him because what they shared is gone. If she continues, she has more to lose—her life. This can work in reverse. She may stop while he continues. Then he fears losing her. He can either stop, try to get her back into the drinking relationship or continue drinking while still trying to hold onto her through abuse.

The shame and degradation a woman feels after being beaten is magnified if she was under the influence of alcohol while it happened. She is not willing to talk about her circumstances because she fears she will be blamed. She is ashamed of being drunk and may blame herself for letting it happen. It is hard enough to admit you are an abused woman, but admitting you are an abused woman with an alcohol problem is far more difficult.

ROBBIE

Robbie came to a shelter after a trip to the emergency room. She was severely abused, physically, sexually and mentally. The first week she could hardly walk, and the women at the shelter took care of her. When she was on her feet and feeling stronger, she started to leave the shelter for errands and job-seeking. One night she did not return to the shelter, but showed up the next morning. She had slept in her car outside the shelter.

This happened more than once and it was finally determined that she had a drinking problem, and that was why she did not return to the shelter at night.

Robbie was confronted about her problem. At first she denied it; then she broke down and admitted there was a problem. The shame she felt from drinking and being abused was devastating. Her drinking problem kept her from working toward her goals. She had no insurance or any income to pay for inpatient treatment. She felt her children were not supportive of her. She thought all they could see was her drinking problem and not the devastation of the abuse she was experiencing. She didn't know where to turn or what problem to try to solve first. She couldn't go back home, yet she had no place to go, no job and no way to support herself.

Women like Robbie are unlikely to seek outside help. If they do seek help, chances are they will seek it for only one of the abuses and ignore the others, at least at first. This makes it difficult for the helper to see the whole scope of the problem and creates problems in working together. The victim may sabotage her own progress because she is not dealing with the total problem. If she works on getting sober and denies the abuse, she risks further abuse, which can lead to more drinking. Or if she works on stopping the abuse and being safe, she may be at risk from her drinking. Either way there are problems to solve, and she remains at risk if she doesn't deal with her total situation.

HER TREATMENT NEEDS

An abused woman who is trying to overcome an addiction is also trying to overcome a life of abuse. Her mate, or abuser, is unlikely to help her overcome these problems. He will not be supportive and instead may work against her. He is losing his mate and may try to do whatever he can to sabotage her progress. This includes not watching the children, withholding support payments, telling lies to friends and family, and taking her house or personal belongings away from her. There are many men who will totally abandon a woman in treatment. It has been reported that as many as 90 percent of husbands leave an alcoholic spouse.

An abused woman does not easily give up the magical thinking that he'll change, the abuse will stop and they can still live a happy life. Her needs to maintain her relationship are strong and likely to be brought into treatment. An abused woman with an alcohol problem may amplify this magical thinking with the thought that when she gets sober, he'll want her back and won't hurt her anymore because he can't blame her anymore for drinking.

This projected outcome is unrealistic. Number one, she is not abused because she is an alcoholic. Violence is about power and control. There is no reason to believe he'll stop abusing her just because she is sober. In fact, an abuser has much to lose when his wife becomes sober. "Deserving" his abuse because of her drunken behavior can no longer serve as an excuse for aggression.

Getting sober solves only some of her problems. The violence was not caused by her being drunk or unable to carry out her family duties. She may have resorted to drinking as a way to cope with and manage an intolerable life, but the consequences only multiplied the abuse and created more problems. Her magical thinking must be confronted and replaced by realistic thinking.

A woman with an addiction problem may be using the drug as her companion or savior. The drug acts as an anesthetic to her pain. The drug can become her best friend, something that will not let her down and will be there for her when she needs it. Breaking this relationship is difficult because she believes her substance to be all that she can depend on to manage her life.

Other complications for the alcohol-abusing woman can include:
- Care for her children while she is in treatment
- General health concerns due to neglecting her own needs
- Other addictions
- Her abusive relationship
- Rebuilding sexuality and body image lost in the addiction process
- Legal concerns
- Financial concerns

- Using support groups
- Family therapy
- Developing relapse prevention skills

This chapter has not covered every aspect of women and alcoholism, only those dimensions relevant to women with an alcohol problem who are also in abusive relationships. The only solution is getting help for both. Your addiction does not excuse mistreatment; it does not alleviate your pain; it does not make it easier to live with yourself; it does not hide your low self-esteem. It merely adds to your problem of being a "hostage in your home." The first step to freedom is sobriety.

AFTERTHOUGHTS

When we were children, we used to think that when we were grown-up we would no longer be vulnerable. But to grow up is to accept vulnerability. . . . To be alive is to be vulnerable.

—Madeleine L'Engle

I believe in recovery, and I believe that as a role model I have the responsibility to let young people know that you can make a mistake and come back from it.

—Former Texas Governor Ann Richards

The best mind-altering drug is truth.

—Lily Tomlin

There can be no happiness if the things we believe in are different from the things we do.

—Freya Stark

We are falling apart inside, and that is why we are falling apart outside.

—Marianne Williamson

VII

GETTING PAST FEAR

Nothing in life is to be feared, it is only to be understood.

—Marie Curie

Asking for help is not easy. On the road to getting help, you will need to dismantle physical and emotional barriers. You must share your personal stories with someone who can listen, understand and help. You have to get in touch with and express your honest feelings. And you will need to change.

LEE ANN: "I FELT I HAD NOWHERE TO GO"

It all started in my childhood. Both my parents drank and when they got drunk they would have a big fight. They would throw things at each other and hit each other. One night I received a phone call from my sister. I was not living at home anymore as I had moved out three months earlier. She was crying and screaming and I couldn't understand what she was saying. Still in my p.j.'s, I jumped in the car and drove to my parents' house.

When I pulled up to the house, I saw police cars and an ambulance there. I ran into the house and saw my mother lying on the floor and paramedics working to revive her. She had been drinking, had a fight with my dad and had taken an overdose of Valium. My sister had been talking on the phone to her and called the ambulance when she realized my mother had passed out. If my sister hadn't called the ambulance, I don't think my mother would be here today. She went to a drug rehabilitation center and got better. Now I am glad to say she doesn't get drunk anymore.

That leads up to my marriage. I married an alcoholic, only I didn't know it at the time I got married. A few months after we were married he got drunk in front of me and got abusive toward me. I was pregnant at the time. I talked to my parents and they wanted me to leave him and get an abortion. There was no way I would not have my baby, so I felt trapped with no place to go.

It's ironic. When I was growing up and my parents fought and my mom got beat up, I thought, "I will never let this happen to me." But I was a child then and had no place else to go. As a married woman, here I was in the same situation. I didn't want this to happen to me, but I felt I had nowhere to go, that I was stuck there just as I was when I was a child.

My husband takes speeders, smokes marijuana and drinks. He can drink anywhere from a 12-pack to a case of beer and not act drunk. Sometimes he becomes very violent. He always says it's my fault. Sometimes maybe it is, but no person deserves to get beat up.

One time he wanted to go to a party by himself and I wanted to go with him. He punched me in the chin and I wound up with three stitches. He told me that I made him hit me. I felt angry and hurt and when he told me it was my fault, I started to feel like maybe it was my fault. After that he was really nice to me; I think he was sorry and felt bad.

Then came the night that I will never, never forget. It was March 25, 1987. It all started when he came home from work. He must have taken a speeder that day because he was grouchy and mean. Nothing I did for him was right. He didn't like the supper, so he started pushing me around. Then he grabbed me by the throat and started to squeeze. He finally let go and went to sit down in the other room, like nothing had ever happened.

I got dressed and went to work so I could get out of the house and let him cool off. He was nice to our little girl. I think he resents me for something that happened to him but I still can't figure out what it could be. So, anyway, I left for work. I was driving home after work and he was coming the opposite way on the road and we met. He had our little girl with him in the car and he tried to run me off the road.

When we got home, he started pushing me, calling me names, and then he slapped me. I hit him back and he threw me on the floor. He still had our little girl in his arms and he put her down and started kicking me.

I remember thinking I was really mad at him for taking our daughter in the car with him. I thought he loved her but now I thought he didn't because how could he take her along to be witness to all this? He jumped on my stomach and started punching me on the top of my head with his fist. I was trying to get him off of me. I scratched his face and he still kept hitting me harder and harder. I was very scared and thought he was going to kill me.

Then all of a sudden I felt something pop and felt something warm running down my head. He stopped hitting me and said, "My God, you're bleeding." I sat up, my head was throbbing, and I looked in the mirror and saw blood running down my forehead. It had started to drip off my eyes. I was dizzy, light-headed and desperate. I went over to the phone to call the police.

My husband grabbed the phone and pulled it out of the wall. I thought he was going to hit me again. He plugged the phone in again and called an ambulance. I had passed out on the floor.

When I got up, he was talking to somebody and telling them how to get here. I stood up and he started toward me. I was scared to death as I didn't know what he would do. I went to the silverware drawer and got out a knife. I wanted to get out of the house. He started to come toward me and I said, "Don't touch me again."

I went out of the house and started up towards the neighbor's, but then I stopped. I didn't want them to see me all bloody. I waited until I saw him come out of the house and snuck back in the back door. I locked the doors so he couldn't get in and waited for the ambulance.

He had put our daughter to bed and I walked down the hall to check on her. I looked at her and she was lying in her crib, looking at the ceiling. She looked scared. I didn't want her to see the blood on my face, so I went to the bathroom to try to clean myself up. There was a knock at the door. It was the paramedics. Boy, was I glad to see them.

When the paramedics saw my head, they called the state police. When they came, my husband lied through his teeth. He told them I came at him with a knife. The police asked me if I wanted to have him arrested and at first I said no, but then I had him arrested because I didn't know what he might do to our daughter. My husband filed charges against me for threatening him with a knife.

I went to the hospital and received three stitches. They said I had a concussion. I was covered with black and blue marks. I felt very hurt and confused. I couldn't believe someone I had married could do this to me. I cried for days about it. I was so angry that I was being arrested for having a knife to protect myself. I had been beat up, I had stitches in my head and I was being arrested! I hated my husband. The police were very nice to me that night.

After I went to the hospital, I went to my parents' house. The next day I went to the women's shelter. I received counseling and friendship, and they helped me realize that it wasn't my fault. I went to a lawyer and got a PFA filed against my husband. That was the best thing I have ever done. I felt good about that.

After he was kicked out and I moved back into the house, he kept calling me. He wouldn't pay me support for myself and our daughter. I threatened to take him to court and he knew I would do it so he finally paid. We went to a marriage counselor but I don't think it did much good.

After three months were up and the PFA expired, he moved back in. I got pregnant and had another child. I feel I can't leave because I don't know how I could take care of and support two children. We have a nice house and I would hate to leave it. My husband is going to counseling and trying. He doesn't drink as much as he used to. He has never laid a hand on me since that day. He knows if he ever hits me again he will go to jail. I will not tolerate being hit ever again. I don't deserve it nor did I cause it; this I know now. I'm taking it one day at a time.

Did Lee Ann receive the kind of help that she needed? Did she solve her problem? Has she found the best solution for her and her daughter? We can all have opinions, but only Lee Ann knows for sure. One thing we do know, however, is that, aware of them or not, there were barriers to her receiving all the help that she needed. For Lee Ann and others like her these barriers consist of an inability to seek help or receive it, often due to fear of retribution, exposure or denial.

WHY I CAN'T ASK FOR HELP

CO-DEPENDENCE

Our co-dependence can be so strong that when degrading or destructive things happen to us, it keeps us from seeing them as negative. We don't see them as positive either. That's just the point: we don't see them at all. Our co-dependent behaviors keep us from asking for help because we are afraid to ask, isolated, not really sure that something is wrong, or we have such a low self-esteem that we do not think we are worthy of intervention.

Moreover, our co-dependence may have started in our childhood as a result of being raised in a dysfunctional family. With this background, we either assume that dysfunctional behaviors occur in all families or we have learned not to ask for help. On the other hand, what may have been learned best by most co-dependents is that when it comes to getting help, other people should get it first. The "good" co-dependent never puts herself first. The "good" co-dependent never gets to treatment either!

ENABLING

Enabling is a delicate issue. To say that a victim enables is to blame the victim. We do not mean that victims contribute to their own victimization. Enabling does not lead to or cause victimization as much as it allows it to continue once it starts. Most enabling behavior was traditionally associated with an alcoholic relationship.

The definition of an enabler is an individual who knowingly or unknowingly does things that permit alcoholic or other dysfunctional behavior to continue without intervention. Although one cannot make another person drink and people do not cause alcoholism in others, one may begin to assume many of the duties and responsibilities of the alcoholic. This can allow the continuation of the dysfunctional behavior and keep the alcoholic from being held responsible. Enabling can raise the enabler's frustration level and can help avoid the confrontation necessary for intervention. Enabling can also keep you from getting help for yourself.

Taking over some or all of the responsibilities of the abuser is an example of enabling. Certainly, you believe you have no choice, but it is this very action that keeps you from meeting your own needs. One example of enabling would be calling the office to say that he won't be in today because he has the flu, when he really has a hangover.

Women who have done that say they feel they have no alternative. If they don't, he may get fired and then where will the money come from? This is true, but consider the other side of it. It won't be as easy for him if he has to make his own calls. If he has to call in himself, he'll have to make the excuses for his behavior and he'll have to deal with the consequences of his drinking.

Enabling rationalizes the problem and allows it to continue. It is a "damned if you do, damned if you don't" dilemma. It is even more delicate when abuse is involved. Any evidence that you are tolerating abuse increases the odds that you will see it happen again.

DENIAL

Denial is the greatest barrier to getting help for yourself. It can work against you in two ways. First, you can deny that a problem or threat exists. Therefore, you need not concern yourself with seeking help. After all, why would you seek help for a problem that doesn't exist? This approach also denies you the right to treatment.

Second, you can admit that the abuse exists but deny that it affects you or that you are bothered by it. Again, you do not go for help. Either way the denial has the same outcome. You and your denial stay home. At the risk of sounding trite, if you want help, you have to admit it before you can get it.

FEAR OF EXPOSURE

Maintaining silence works against your getting help. If you are uncertain about revealing your problem to others, ask yourself, "What is the worst thing that could happen to me if others know what is happening?" Whatever your answer, is it as fearful as continuing in an abusive relationship?

What actually happens after the secret is exposed depends on whom you share the secret with and under what conditions. People who genuinely want to help you will support your sharing. Those who may make you uncomfortable or judge you are not the people in whom you should confide anyway.

FEAR OF RETALIATION

You say you'd like to leave, at least for a while, but you're afraid of what he might do then. He's already threatened to do something rash, like tell his parents or yours that you've left him for another man. The fear cycle is always the same: "What will he do if I go for help or leave?" He has threatened you before and you know the damage he can do. Many women have said that their husbands threatened to "really hurt" them if they left. Fear of being defenseless against false accusations or against superior physical power can keep us from acting in our own best interests.

This fear of retaliation or retribution cannot only immobilize us, it can also blind us to a broader outlook on our lives. In other words, you are too afraid of what may happen to you if you leave to be able to assess and trust the benefits of asking for help. Your outlook is dominated by fear, not by hope. An example of how this might come about is revealed in the following story.

ANN: SHE SHARED HER FEARS

Ann, a 24-year-old, was married, had a full time job, two children and was the sole support for her family. Her husband had lost his job in the mines over a year before and had not been able to find work since. He watched the children while she went to work. Every day when she came home from work, her husband would ask her to whom she talked during the day. She worked for a man and was in a predominantly male environment. Therefore, most of her conversations were with men. Her husband would get furious and accuse her of having affairs, being unfaithful and wanting other men besides him.

Every day she would tell him that talking to men was unavoidable and part of her job. She would try to reassure him that he was the only man in her life. Sometimes she would have to be with him at that very moment in order to prove that she meant what she said.

As time passed, Ann began to feel quite apprehensive when she returned home from work. One day she told her husband that if he couldn't believe her, she would leave so he could find another woman whom he felt could be faithful to him. Her husband's reaction was to take down one of the guns off the wall in the living room, point it at her and threaten to shoot.

She was terrified. She grabbed the child nearest her and ran out the door. He chased her into the yard but did not follow her down the street as she ran to her mother-in-law's house. What was she to do now? He had a gun, had been drinking and had the other child with him in the house. Would he hurt her child? She didn't think so but could not rule out that fear.

Her main concerns at that moment were how to get back into the house, get her child and gather her belongings so she could go to work the next day. Her mother-in-law offered to talk to him. She didn't understand what was going on between them, but was distressed and didn't want Ann to be unable to go to work the next day. She talked to her son and told Ann that he would let her come back home. He denied to his mother the threats with the gun.

Ann went back home because she felt there was no real alternative at the time. When she went into the house, he informed her that he would always keep the children, so she could never leave and take the children with her. Her attempts to stand up to him were met with severe retaliation. He also threatened to call her boss and tell him to stay away from his wife or else he would come into the office and thrash him.

Ann came to the women's shelter during her lunch hour. She conveyed her story and fears of what he might do next. We discussed options that she suggested. Under the circumstances they were few. One option was to tell his mother the whole story in hopes that she would talk to him. He thought highly of his mother's opinions and he might listen to her. The more we discussed this, the more Ann thought it would not be helpful. His mother thought her son could "do no wrong" and this might just stir up more tension between Ann and her.

Another option was to leave. Ann had friends at work who were willing to help her. In fact, one friend had offered to move her to a vacant apartment he knew was available. Ann's main worries about this option were how she was going to get her children and belongings out of the house, and what her husband would do to her and to her friends if he found out that they helped her.

Ann's lunch hour was over and she had to return to work. We had written down the options with the intention that she was to add to the list if she thought of any other possibilities. She would come back tomorrow and talk again, this time joining the women's support group.

She returned the next day and told the women's group her story and her desire to leave. She also shared her fears of what he might do to her, her children or her friends. The group supported her concerns and shared their own personal stories. Their questions to her were, "What will happen if you continue to live in this environment? Will his retaliations for your leaving be worse than what you're living with now?" The group also stressed that her husband had already threatened Ann's life. They asked her, "If you're dead, who'll care for your children? What's more important, your happiness and well-being (your life, for that matter) or his domination and control?"

Ann needed to hear this and needed to hear it from people who were primarily concerned for her personal well-being. The caring atmosphere in which these concerns were conveyed strengthened Ann's conviction to act for her personal safety.

The fear of retribution or retaliation can work against trying to do something to change an abusive situation. Fears can immobilize you and prevent you from taking positive action. It is always "the known versus the unknown." It is not easy to see the opposite side of what it would be like if you asked for help when you are too emotionally involved to see beyond your immediate situation.

The clearer picture can sometimes be seen by those who are not emotionally bound to the problem—a friend or trained helper. Fear, too, has a way of keeping us from acting in our best interests. Bringing the fear into the open, discussing it with a concerned and emotionally uninvolved person, and pursuing "what if's?" may provide you with the tools to act in your own best interests and overcome the fear of retaliation.

Fear of Making It Worse

Are you afraid you will do something that will make things worse? You say, "Things aren't going well, but they could be worse." That's exactly what they do, they get worse. Do you honestly believe that by doing nothing you will "freeze" your relationship where it is? Think about where your relationship was a few years ago. It probably is worse today. If you do nothing, where will you be a few years from now? Perhaps you're thinking it has been this way for years. However, both abuse and alcoholism are progressive. They will not stop or go backwards by themselves.

Are you the same person you were several years ago? Do you have the same level of self-esteem, the same attitude toward your life, the same parenting skills, the same hope for the future? Your fear of making it worse becomes self-fulfilling when you do nothing.

We know you're afraid he will become more abusive if you do something, but he is becoming more abusive anyway. Unfortunately your inactivity does not stop his. You can try to hold on while he gets worse, until maybe you reach the point where you can no longer tolerate what he is doing. But while you're waiting, you risk becoming unable to help yourself.

Self-blame

Many women in abusive relationships do not go for help because they believe they are partly to blame. To blame for what? Being abused? Being verbally and emotionally assaulted? You are not the cause of these things, you are the victim!

It is not so much your behaviors that convince you that you are to blame as it is the way you think about the abuse and your relationships. Thoughts such as "It's my responsibility to keep the relationship happy and together" and "If anything is wrong it's my fault" reinforce your self-blame. Statements such as "I couldn't figure out what I was doing that made him so mad" or "No matter how hard I tried, I just couldn't make it right" are typical when you begin to blame yourself for the problems you endure.

Blaming yourself can keep you from asking for help because you believe it is not "justified." For example, if you believe you have anything to do with causing the abuse, as long as you deny the abuse you can simultaneously deny you had anything to do with causing it. You conduct a trial in your mind that concludes, "As long as abuse doesn't exist, I am not guilty of causing it."

Overcoming self-blame means that you no longer accept his excuses for his behavior. It also means that you raise your opinion of yourself and that you establish boundaries about the kinds of responsibilities you will and won't accept. Allowing someone else to make you feel responsible for his problems is an indicator of how severe a problem it has become for you. You did not cause the abuse. You have endured the abuse. Don't accept either the blame or the abuse.

Assuming No One Wants to Help

Do you assume that since you are so unique or isolated that no help exists for you? Do you realize that these are the same feelings other abused women have? There are millions of women in abusive relationships. It is one of the largest groups of "unique" people we have ever met.

The more you believe that you are different, the higher the probability you think that no one can help you or that there is not an agency for your "particular" problem. In America today, you name it and there is a support group for it. To get started you must find one and ask for help. All the personal stories in this book are from women who believed there was no help. Now, most of them are trying to help others, even if only by sharing their stories in order to let you know that you are not alone.

Assuming there is no support is also based on a "what's the use?" attitude. You believe that no one can help, that nothing will change and that everything is hopeless. This attitude, and the belief that you are unique, keeps you not only from supporting yourself, but also from receiving the support of others. Like so many assumptions that dominate abusive relationships, these, too, are false. Help is available. People do care about you. Problems can be solved. You can recover, but you must make yourself available to the help that exists. Doing nothing keeps you isolated. Just as you tell your children to try the food they say they don't want, you must try the support systems; you may like it.

All barriers, whether real or imaginary, can keep you from getting help. For many women, working through these barriers is a prerequisite to finding a solution to abuse. Do not allow your fears of getting help to keep you living in fear. Go for help now.

AFTERTHOUGHTS

You can live a lifetime and, at the end of it, know more about other people than you know about yourself.

—Beryl Markham

It is never too late to be what you might have been.

—George Eliot

You don't get to choose how you are going to die or when. You can only decide how you're going to live.

—Joan Baez

A story is told as much by silence as it is by speech.

—Susan Griffin

If you are not afraid of the voices inside you, you will not fear the critics outside you.

—Natalia Ginzburg

VIII

GETTING HELP FOR ABUSE

Whatever you want in your life, other people are going to want too. Believe in yourself enough to accept the idea that you have an equal right to it.

—Diane Sawyer

There are many resources to help you cope with the problems stemming from your abusive relationship. In this chapter we will discuss five specific kinds of help that are available. Begin your search for help with one of these. While they do not represent all the help that is out there, they are a good place to begin. Be aware that there is an overlap in the types of help different resources provide. It may not be so much a matter of which one you choose, but that you begin somewhere. If one source does not meet your needs, try another. Don't give up. You might give up on a particular agency or an approach, but do not give up on your quest for help.

WOMEN'S SHELTERS

Abused women's shelters are an excellent source of help. They understand victims of violence and are informed about the full spectrum of helping resources in your community. The abuser cannot get to you while you are there, so he can't pressure you to return to him or put anybody else in jeopardy. You will receive support and can take your time to rest, feel safe and make decisions in an unpressured environment. You can make plans, get answers to your questions and obtain referrals to appropriate helping sources.

Beyond separation, protection, security and referrals to helping sources, abused women's shelters promote the formation of bonds with other women. There are usually several women and their children at the shelter at all times. You will meet women like yourself and discover that you are not alone. Your isolation and secrecy can be broken and you will find that there is hope. By talking with other women, you will learn how they got out and what they did to help themselves.

Women in shelters lend support to each other. They watch each other's children, share the cooking and housekeeping duties at the shelter, and form a camaraderie of which you will be a part. Some women who meet in shelters eventually decide to live together to reduce living expenses.

The staff provides role models. Some are former abused women themselves. They have worked with many abused women and share success stories to provide encouragement. They provide education and supportive counseling. The staff and abused woman work together as peers, and the battered woman is considered to be the expert on what she needs. She is no longer a helpless victim. She experiences success in making her own decisions and following through on them. She gains a sense of control and power over her life.

If you do not know of a shelter in your community, ask any social service agency where the nearest one is located. Church leaders, government officials or women's services can give you this information. There may be a shelter in a nearby community or county. There may be a domestic violence hotline you can call for help. Keep asking until you get the answers you need.

Besides direct services, a shelter offers the opportunity to belong, to be accepted and supported, to be free from blame and, most important, a chance to think of yourself first. These are the exact opposite characteristics of those in an abusive relationship. These may be new to you. You may even feel uncomfortable expressing yourself. Remember, however, that it has been a long time since you shared your needs and hopes. Give the shelter experience some time. Give yourself some time. You are worth it.

WOMEN'S GROUPS

Women's groups for abused spouses are a valuable source of support. The best place to break down barriers of isolation and uniqueness is in a group. Being with other people who can offer assistance, advice and support is better than being alone in fear, loneliness and despair. Women's groups focus on women's concerns. You may need to know that what you feel is common to other women and that you have a right to be cared for, reassured, nurtured and supported. A women's support group can fulfill these needs as nothing else can.

Sharing is the agenda, to help all or one. You will not be told what to do. You make your own decisions, but hearing how another solved her problems can give you hope and confidence. The atmosphere of a healthy support group conveys love, care and genuine mutual support.

Assertiveness, child-rearing and single women's problems are addressed and alternative solutions explored. Role models emerge, common bonds form and self-esteem improves through this process of exchange.

Domestic violence shelters, mental health centers, drug and alcohol prevention units, church groups and community health centers are some of the places that may sponsor women's groups or can tell you how to find one. With the group you are never alone. Just as some resources may not meet your needs, not all groups will be right for you. If you go to a group and feel that your needs are not being met, try another group. It may be that in the first group, people and issues did not match up. This does not negate the value of groups. Keep trying until you find the group that you can grow in.

SOCIAL SERVICES

Social services provide support for independent living. Public assistance, child protective services, housing information and assistance, fuel assistance programs, Social Security, family planning and food programs are a few of the many services available. Mental health clinics and drug and alcohol centers can offer help to the entire family.

A word of caution: if the worker is not informed about family violence issues, find another source. Social services are becoming more aware of family violence and many will go out of their way to help an abused woman. Find the sources that are supportive to you. Community mental health centers, drug and alcohol centers, church leaders, public officials and hospital social workers are sources of information that can point you in the right direction.

Social services are particularly important because we realize that you may have other problems besides the abuse. Rarely do we find only one problem in an abusive relationship. Depending on your circumstances you may benefit from receiving help from several agencies.

LAWYERS

Lawyers or Legal Aid can advise you of your legal rights. This is particularly important since many victims only speculate about their rights. Discussions go on for hours about what they think they can or cannot do. We always recommend against speculating or using second-hand information. Consult a legal professional to get accurate information.

If the abuser threatens to take your children away from you, refuses child support, won't accept a divorce or physically threatens you, find out exactly what your rights are. If you are seeking support, separation or divorce, a lawyer's help is clearly a necessity. Regardless of the severity of the problem, knowing your rights gives you power and reduces intimidation from your partner. These matters are too serious to rely on hearsay.

Besides knowing your legal rights, you should understand exactly what steps you can take to protect them. For example, protection for a woman and her children in the form of a Protection From Abuse (PFA) order is provided by legal services. For women who can't afford a private lawyer, there are legal services available supported by the community and private organizations.

Countless women have told us of the physical or legal threats their husbands have made, what they said they would and could do if the women left them. Once the women understood their legal rights, they knew that many of the threats could not be carried out. A woman gains a sense of empowerment when she knows her legal rights and has someone to stand up for them.

Many communities offer legal assistance based on one's income. These services may be limited, but most of them at least offer PFA orders. Call and ask what legal services community agencies offer and to whom these services are available. Private attorneys' fees and payment plans vary widely. Call attorneys and ask them about their rates.

Ask the community social workers about their experiences with various lawyers. Above all, ask other women in similar circumstances. These sources can provide advice in finding a lawyer who is right for you. Remember, if you are dissatisfied with your lawyer's response to you and your problem, you have the right to find another. Having a lawyer is having legal protection. Do not leave yourself unprotected.

FRIENDS AND FAMILY

Friends and family members can provide both emotional and physical support. Some people won't understand but others will. Even if they don't understand, some will be willing to lend a hand.

Perhaps a friend has a place you can stay while you find more permanent housing. Clothing, household items and money may be some of your urgent needs, and a friend or family member may be willing to help. We have found that people are very giving to others who need help. The shelter where Susan worked received many calls with offers of clothing, stoves, refrigerators, couches and the like. People will help others in need. All they want is a chance to show their care and concern.

It is sometimes difficult for abused women to ask for help because they're unaccustomed to asking. However, the other side of giving is receiving. Part of changing positively is learning to ask and receive as well as to give. Often a woman thinks she must give and ask for nothing in return. It doesn't work that way; she needs to know how to get her own needs met, too. This involves asking others for help. They cannot be expected to know what she needs from them.

A word of advice to the abused woman: *TALK TO SOMEONE ABOUT YOUR PROBLEMS.* If you are an abused woman and search out a friend, family member or a professional to tell your story to, you are taking the first gigantic step toward helping yourself. You are breaking the isolation. You are not keeping the secret any longer. You will find that some people will understand and some won't. The important thing to remember is that there are many people who will understand. You simply have to find them. You have broken out of the prison of secrecy and shame. You will find you are not alone.

When you tell your story, you can sense if people will be helpful by their reactions. If they believe you and disapprove of abuse, you have found a supportive source. If they react otherwise, find another source. Don't give up. You've let the secret out, so continue to talk. The more people you talk to, the more support you will find. Some people will be willing to take a risk and help you. These people are your true support systems. Remember, they made the choice to help; you haven't forced them. They may be taking risks, but it's their decision.

When your abuser sees that you are receiving help, he may react by threatening you and the people who help you. But he also sees that people are willing to help you, he is not all-powerful and you have the right to live without abuse anymore.

The most disheartening thing to people who help abused women is to see them go back to the abuser. If this happens in your case, they must remember that it is your life. Your reasons can be overwhelming. Remind them that you won't go back as the same person you were before you left. You know you have rights, you know you can leave again and you know there are people who disapprove of your being abused.

The confusion an abused woman may face within herself is over why she would return to her abuser. You have found people who support your right to live a life free from abuse. You're probably returning because you think your old life will change. Regardless of what happens, you yourself have changed. You know that the abuse was not your fault, you did not cause him to abuse you and you have rights. How you choose to live now is your decision.

You have choices that may not be the ones you would have chosen, but there are options just the same. Your life has changed because you see it differently. You will have to make some ultimatums to yourself about how you want to live and how you want your children to live.

Still, nothing works unless you convince your spouse that you mean business and that you will follow through with what you say. You can't convince your spouse until you yourself are convinced that you are willing and able to follow through with what you say. This is the bottom line. The changes occur within the relationship when the changes occur within you.

THE SUPPORT YOU SHOULD RECEIVE

It is crucial that your needs are recognized and supported by the people or agencies trying to help you. Regardless of the type of support system that you choose, there are seven issues that must be addressed in nearly every case of abuse.

BREAKING THROUGH YOUR ISOLATION

The helper must be able to help you break through the isolation you feel. A good helper will let you tell your story. This person must realize that she or he may be the first person you told or may be the first person who has let you talk freely. Conveying the message to you that it's all right to talk and that someone is listening communicates that you can talk in an accepting atmosphere. Your actions should not be judged, but understood. Also, helpers should not judge your abuser. This places them in the role of accuser instead of helper.

You, like other abused women, might tell your story in bits and pieces. You may be testing the helper, trying to figure out just how much you can tell, closely watching for reactions to each thing you say. On the other hand, your story may come rushing out full of emotions and painful recounts of abuse. You should be allowed to take your time and tell it in your own way. The focus should be kept on you.

It's necessary to share the truth about the kinds of abuse you have endured, but it's just as important to share your feelings about your reactions and responses. The helper is working with you and needs to hear about your reactions and feelings more than anyone else's. We always tell a woman we are working with that we can't do anything to make someone else change his actions. All we can do is focus on her and what she can do for herself to make the situation change. While breaking through your isolation you should begin to feel less alone, and that you are beginning to be supported.

AFFIRMING YOUR RIGHT NOT TO BE ABUSED

No one deserves to be beaten or abused in any way! No one! You should hear this message repeatedly when you go for help. It should be reinforced that you do not deserve abusive treatment and that you did not cause it. Statements such as "You didn't deserve such treatment" or "You were not the reason he abused you" reaffirm your right to be treated with respect and dignity.

Another right that treatment should affirm for you is that you have a right to the treatment itself. It should be affirmed that you were deeply affected and that it is normal for you to want to get help. Wanting to get help, going for treatment and desiring to improve the quality of your life are all affirmations that you have a right to be here, and more important, that you have a right to recover. Exercise your rights!

HELPING YOU IDENTIFY AND UNDERSTAND YOUR ANGER

There is tremendous anger, often unrecognized, within an abused woman. It may be too scary for you to acknowledge this anger because you're afraid you do not know how to handle it. Anger toward the abuser can take passive/aggressive forms. You may not confront the abuser directly, but act indirectly to show your anger. An example would be your wanting to use the car and him telling you that you don't need to go anywhere. Knowing his car is his pride and joy, you throw dirt on it in retaliation. He sees the car later with dirt on it, becomes upset, and rants and raves about how it could have happened and who did it. You maintain that you don't know a thing about it. He blames the kids but you never say a word about it.

Anger can be expressed more aggressively. You can take it out on someone else, such as your children or friends. For example, one woman in the shelter was upset with her mother for not watching the kids for her while she went to work. Her husband being home while she was at work, and therefore being able to watch the kids, was not the issue to her. She talked instead of how she was angry with her mother for not helping her and how it was her mother's fault she had to get a sitter, having to pay a big chunk of her salary for childcare. Actually, she was angry at her husband for not helping out, but didn't dare direct her anger at him. She was also frustrated because she could not save enough money to get out of the marriage. It was too frightening for her to vent her anger at him, so she vented her anger and outrage at her mother, a safer target.

The most debilitating way for an abused woman to demonstrate her anger is to turn it against herself. She gets angry at herself for everything she does, blames herself and feels she is worthless. This destroys her self-esteem and feeds into her victim role. You need a place to express your anger, somewhere you can work through it. Moreover, you should feel that expressing your anger is appropriate and that you are not being told to subvert or deny your anger. A good helper or helping agency will recognize the anger you feel and help you release it.

EDUCATING YOU ABOUT ABUSE AS A SERIOUS SOCIAL PROBLEM

When you go for help, abuse should be recognized for exactly what it is. No matter what its form, denial or rationale, it is abuse. Part of any intervention is receiving what is called "affective" education. This provides maximum information about your situation, helping you to see the abuse more clearly. You should receive information about all forms of abuse, both to understand and help you work through your own situation and to recognize your choices.

A major weapon used by the abuser against the woman is controlling her access to information. We have seen this time and again when the woman wants to go for help. He tells her, "You don't need that," or "Nobody will listens to you" or "How can anyone tell us what's wrong with our relationship?" You have a right to become as knowledgeable as possible about your abuse and to use this knowledge to help yourself. Make sure that you are receiving help from knowledgeable people and do not be afraid to ask questions.

HELPING YOU OVERCOME YOUR GUILT

It is amazing how you often can be a victim and still feel guilty. Your sources of guilt can be many, but you need to understand them all. Your guilt can involve feeling sorry for him, feeling he needs you, feeling you should not be sharing the relationship secret, believing that you have caused the problem, feeling you are abandoning him or hoping he'll change. Justified or not, the guilt does not disappear by itself.

You need help to understand how these messages developed. Your need to feel important and to be needed instead of being manipulated and made to feel guilty must be established. Staying with an abusive man because he needs you has to be considered from the standpoint of whose needs are being met and whose are not. There is a difference between being needed by someone because you are special and provide love and encouragement, and being needed by someone who expects you to fulfill his every abusive expectation and meet his every need.

Guilt is a difficult barrier to overcome. If you leave, the abuser will make many promises to get you back. He apologizes, says he'll never hurt you again, tells you he can't live without you or even threatens to kill himself if you don't return. All this fuels your guilt. You can be overwhelmed. The guilt was there before you went for help, it was there while you received help and it can still be there while you are trying to make changes.

Make sure that you are getting the necessary support for working through the guilt. If you do not receive help for it, you can stop the abuse, but the guilt will probably remain. It is possible to change your life externally by leaving or stopping the abuse, but internally your guilty feelings may linger unresolved. You deserve better than this and should be informed of your options, given choices and encouraged to act in new ways to help free yourself from the burden of guilt.

GIVING YOU YOUR OWN TIME AND SPACE

The abused woman needs time away from the abuser to work things out. She should be encouraged to take some time for herself, to rest and to think about her situation and how she might make it better. If the abuser can't contact her and she can take time for herself without pressure from him, she can work through some of her anger and guilt and reconsider her options. Too often she does not allow herself the time needed to work this through and returns to the abuser. Once she's back with him, she'll again be pressured to see things his way.

Whoever is helping you can play an important role in allowing you time to think and talk in a supportive environment. Not allowing your abuser access to this environment is essential. This is where shelters can be effective, as they will not allow your abuser contact or access to you.

Friends and family are at greater risk. The abuser may plead with them and eventually make his influence felt. It will take strength and courage for them to stand up to him. If they resist by not helping him gain access to you, they will pass a supreme test of friendship and show they truly care. Again and again women tell stories of not being able to stay with friends or receive their help because the friends didn't want to become involved in a domestic dispute. This is not a domestic dispute; this is the safety and well-being of a woman who needs help. If you are supported by others, you will know you are not alone. Other people standing up for your rights as a person, acting against something that is wrong and intolerable, demonstrate that you have a right not to be abused.

Supporting Your Decisions

The victim must make many decisions after she leaves. The picture is awesome and filled with complications. Often she is unable to make such a crucial decision as staying in or leaving the relationship right away. She may need time to rest, heal and explore alternatives. Whatever decisions she makes must be her own.

You should not be told what to do; rather, you should receive support for your decisions. You can be told what options you have and explore outcomes from each, but the decision is solely yours to make. You need to get out of the helpless or victim role and into one where you have control. You need to build self-confidence by doing things for yourself. You need to experience the success and positive feelings this self-sufficiency will give you. You need support in whatever you decide.

If someone else makes your decisions for you, you will remain helpless even though you are trying to change. Support is different from doing it for you. Support involves giving you information on available sources of help, helping you with your feelings and facilitating your recovery. The best support you can receive from a helper is getting to the point where you no longer need her or him for your decisions. You will then have gained control over your life.

We realize that many abuse problems entail immediate needs and amount to a crisis. While you are getting help, be sure to address immediate needs such as your health, a plan for safety, your emotions, housing, financial assistance, employment and a contingency plan in the event that abuse recurs. Getting help will depend upon not only the issues discussed in this chapter, but also upon the kinds of responses and help that you perceive you need right now. Remember, however, that in order to get help you have to ask.

AFTERTHOUGHTS

Not to transmit an experience is to betray it.

—Elie Wiesel

Although the world is full of suffering, it is full also of the overcoming of it.

—Helen Keller

What one has to do usually can be done.

—Eleanor Roosevelt

You may be disappointed if you fail, but you are doomed if you don't try.

—Beverly Sills

"Hope" is the thing with feathers
That perches in the soul—
And sings the tune without words
And never stops—at all.

—Emily Dickinson

IX

DRINKING PROBLEMS NEED HELP, TOO

In grief we know the worst of what we feel,
But who can tell the end of what we fear?

—Hannah More

He's addicted to alcohol and you're addicted to him. Somebody needs help—namely, you. We are not concerned in this chapter with getting help for his addiction, although we hope that all alcoholics will seek treatment. This book is about you and your recovery. As stated in Chapter Five, people who live with problem drinkers are intimately involved with someone who is creating problems for them. These problems compromise your self-esteem, parenting skills, relationship skills and your emotional intimacy with others. Overcoming these problems requires recovery.

Your feelings of being harmed by your relationship with an alcoholic are not unique. Since 1951, millions of spouses of alcoholics have sought help through Al-Anon, a support network designed to help the nonalcoholic spouse and family members overcome the effects of exposure to alcoholism. While not exclusively a women's program, Al-Anon has helped many women help themselves and has consistently reinforced the message that they have a right to treatment. And, it's free.

Recovery from alcoholism is not just for the alcoholic. If it were, you would again find yourself dependent upon him for what you need. He has dominated you enough. Never allow his unwillingness to seek treatment to dictate whether or not you seek help. It is unfortunate to have to live with an alcoholic; it is far worse to be unable to do anything about it when the alcoholic will not stop drinking. This is codependency at its worst. Your recovery comes first!

Your recovery from alcoholism will depend upon many events and circumstances. We will discuss several of them in this chapter. As you read, it is important to maintain a positive frame of reference about yourself. The following are beliefs you must accept in order to start on the road to recovery from exposure to alcohol abuse:

- You have a right to recovery
- Your recovery comes first; his comes second
- You can recover from alcoholism
- You do not have to recover alone
- Recovery takes time, and the best way to take it is one day at a time
- You did not cause the alcoholism
- You cannot control the drinking
- You cannot get sober for him

Many of the helpful avenues open to victims of abuse are also available to victims of exposure to someone else's alcoholism. Also, many of the same emotions—denial, guilt, shame, embarrassment and fear—that must be confronted in getting help for abuse are present when you seek help for yourself in response to a spouse's alcoholism. However, just as physically and psychologically abusive relationships have their own special characteristics, so do alcohol abusing relationships. The following topics highlight how you can recover from his drinking problem. Remember to keep the focus on yourself!

ALCOHOLIZING: THE MAGICAL CURE

"If only he would quit drinking, everything would be fine" is the stuff of which "magical cures" for the alcoholic relationship are made. This type of thinking has several implications for your recovery. One, it puts recovery on hold as long as he is still drinking. Two, it assumes that all of your relationship problems are caused by his drinking and by nothing else. Three, it assumes that you are going to the "promised relationship land" if and when he recovers. This type of thinking means that you have "alcoholized" all the problems in your relationship: you blame all your problems on the drinking.

What if he does stop drinking? Does that make you a recovering person? Is that a guarantee that he will no longer be abusive? You have been exposed to alcoholism and you have a right to overcome the effects of that exposure. Taking the alcohol away does not take away your history of exposure. Your recovery involves overcoming any negative effects you have suffered from the time you were involved with a problem drinker. Rejecting or ignoring this implies a belief that the magical cure will not only cure him, but even if you do nothing yourself, it will also cure you! It doesn't work that way.

Forgo your belief in the magical cure and start believing in yourself. Don't become co-dependent upon this magical belief; become dependent upon your own rational beliefs.

WAITING FOR THE SOBRIETY STORK

When sobriety is "delivered" everything will go away, you will be fine and the two of you will live happily ever after. This kind of thinking begs several questions. What makes you think that he is going to get sober? We know: he promised. Can you wait that long? There is no official length of pregnancy for the sobriety stork, and most of the time it doesn't arrive when you want it. Does waiting for his sobriety mean that you cannot help yourself? Usually, while the nonalcoholic partner is waiting, relationships become strained or emotionally devastated, children grow up under stress and the non-alcoholic begins to change in undesirable ways.

If he does get sober, should you still go for help? Yes. Remember that you were exposed to alcoholism and have a right to overcome its effects on you. When the sobriety stork arrives, it only delivers. It doesn't take anything away. Your recovery will be a process of learning to let some of the negative effects go, accepting yourself as you are now and becoming the person you would like to be.

BREAK YOUR ISOLATION

Share your feelings and share the "relationship secret." Keeping it to yourself keeps all the pain in, and people who could help you out. There are many programs and people who will help. They cannot help you if they cannot find you. Keeping you isolated is exactly what he would like to do. You are easier to control when you are without support. You may believe that you have handled his drinking by yourself, but in reality you have been handled by his drinking.

Allow yourself to share with others by putting yourself into a position to share. Break your isolation by seeking out women's groups, other support groups and alcohol treatment agencies, and by sharing your experiences and concerns. You will be surprised to find that you are not the only person who has tried to handle it alone and only ended up lonely.

"DON'T BLAME ME"

Wouldn't you like to tell him where he can go when he blames you for everything, including his drinking? Part of your recovery involves freeing yourself from being blamed for his drinking. Only a co-dependent will accept blame for someone else's behavior. How does he think you caused his drinking? Did you go to the liquor store, buy the alcohol, find him, physically hold him down and pour the alcohol into his body until he became addicted? Remember, you didn't cause it. You can't control it. You are not going to accept the blame for it.

HOME REMEDIES

Whatever they are, they don't work. Go to treatment, please.

THE DEFINITION DEBATE

About the time that many women can no longer tolerate his drinking and are thinking about going for help we often hear, "Maybe he isn't alcoholic and maybe I don't need any help." After all you have been through with his drinking, this is no time to start a mental debate. Even if you do not think or want to admit that he is an alcoholic, there is no denying that his drinking and associated behaviors are causing problems for you. Problem drinking is a stage on the way to becoming alcoholic. Besides, you are the one that we are concerned about, and if his drinking is causing problems for you, then you have problems and should go for help.

Don't wait for him to be "officially" diagnosed as alcoholic. Unfortunately, only 20 percent of alcoholics go for help even once (Ackerman 1987). Therefore, the majority of alcoholics are never officially recognized. That means you must recognize what alcoholism is and how it can affect you. This is not easy for many women to do, and it appears to be even more difficult for them to go for help. In a national study of people who were raised in alcoholic families it was found that only 11 percent of non-alcoholic spouses had gone for help (Ackerman 1987). You cannot wait for him to get help. You pay too high a price while you wait.

LEARN THE FACTS ABOUT ALCOHOLISM

We know that you are living with it, but how much do you actually know about the disease of alcoholism? It is extremely difficult to recover from something without fully understanding what you are trying to work through. The more knowledge you have about alcoholism and its effects on you, the better prepared you will be to seek alternatives and to facilitate your own recovery. Learn about the stages of alcoholism, how it progresses, how it destroys relationships and how it affects the alcoholic and those around him or her physically, emotionally and spiritually. Above all, learn about recovery, the steps involved and how to become a recovering person.

Do you know what types of resources and programs are available to you in your community to help recover from alcoholism? Have you called an alcohol treatment program and talked to someone? Explore all the alternatives. The more you can discover, the wider your range of choices and the better your chance for a full recovery.

MAKE PEACE WITH REALITY

Making peace with reality will be one of the first steps in your recovery process. You will put aside your denial and see the situation for what it is: someone else's drinking has caused problems for you. Making peace with reality requires admitting that alcoholism exists, that you have been affected, that you want help, that help is available and that you will seek it. In order to do this you will need to break through denial. Learn to let go of the "if only" syndrome. Stop wishing that it would be different and do something about it.

Do not confuse acceptance of reality with approval. You do not have to approve of everything you accept about your relationship. We do not approve of abusive or alcoholic relationships, but we accept that they exist. We do not approve of the alcoholic's adverse effect on other people, but we accept that it occurs.

Not everyone's reality will be the same. What does it mean to you to be in a relationship with a problem drinker? What are you admitting to yourself if you say that your partner is alcoholic? Does this mean that you are admitting:

- You have overcome denial?

- Your partner has a drinking problem and that it is creating problems for you?

- You have come to terms with the word "alcoholic" and all that it implies?

- You feel as if you have betrayed someone by acknowledging it?

- You are going to say good-bye to the image of the partner you have and see him as he actually is?

- You might not be normal if you admit you live in an abnormal situation?

- You would like help?

- You must confront the alcoholic?

- Your relationship will fall apart and you think he will leave you?

- You blame yourself for his drinking?

Not everyone's reality is the same. Some of the above implications may apply to you, but only you can know what it means to you to be in your situation. If you can accept and make peace with your reality, you will no longer fear it.

THE AWARENESS TRAP

Be cautious of the awareness trap as you enter your recovery. This can happen if you become so engrossed in the "process" of recovery that you forget the end product. You learn all about the steps and procedures for recovery, you have read all the material, you are aware of how you should be, but you have never understood why or how to live your recovery. You only know that you should be open, honest and free, but you do not know what for. You can get caught in the trap of becoming aware, but unable to apply that awareness to your life.

There is a big difference between knowing and doing. To recover is a verb. In the awareness trap you go through the motions at the expense of your emotions. Raising your level of awareness about your life and about all your alternatives is a step in recovery. Do not confuse it with recovery itself.

FIND A HEALTHY GROUP

There are many different types of self-help groups with which you can become involved during your recovery. If you go to a group and it doesn't meet your needs, try another group or another type of group. There are five important reasons why self-help groups are likely to promote the growth of individual members.

1. Each member can use the resources of the entire group.
2. Just as "the whole is greater than the sum of its parts," the combined experiences and solutions found in a group are greater than what is known by only one person.
3. Each member remains her own best authority on what she needs and what can work for her.
4. Being with other people is the best way to break through isolation and feelings of uniqueness.
5. Millions of people have been helped in self-help groups.

How do you know what to look for in seeking a "healthy" group? According to Frank Reissman (1984), the director of the National Self-Help Clearinghouse, these are some of the distinctive features of healthy self-help groups:

- A shared commitment and cohesiveness
- Not standing still but adding new members, allowing the older members to play more of a helper role
- A strong norm of giving help, evenly distributed throughout the group

- A shared and distributed leadership of various kinds, both formal and informal
- An ideology or rationale that explains the problem they are addressing and the methodology for coping with it
- Dealing with a strongly felt need, problem or illness
- Definite traditions and structure
- A strong experiential knowledge base
- A good balance between the informal, open ethos and the structured dimension related to continuity, group maintenance and follow-up
- Realistic approaches to problems of relapse or regression
- A belief in themselves; a belief that they are effective in dealing with the problems and needs of members
- A relationship with a national organization, such as AA, Recovery, Inc., Parents Anonymous, even if the relationship is loose and informal

A good group experience means finding a healthy group and participating to the fullest. Do not join a group that monitors your behavior rigidly. You do not want to attempt to recover from the control of your partner by joining an organization that is equally controlling. You do not want to be in a group that does your thinking for you. After all, learning to think for yourself again is one of the main reasons you joined the group in the first place.

Beware of being too dependent upon the group at the risk of not developing your own identity. Your membership in a support group is to assist you during your crisis and to support your growth. The group cannot do it for you. A healthy group will not try to control you, but will help you to help yourself make the right decisions.

JOIN AL-ANON

We strongly recommend that women who are in a relationship with a problem drinker join Al-Anon. Al-Anon assists the nonalcoholic partner's or family members' recovery from the experience of living with alcoholism. In Al-Anon the focus is on you. You will hear how to better take care of yourself and you will receive help with your feelings. Moreover, the program will teach you how to live at peace with yourself. You will find, perhaps for the first time, that you belong and that you and your issues are accepted. Al-Anon is not only a self-help program, it is a part of a "recovering community." You can belong to this community. It offers all the features of what a healthy group should be and its traditions are strong.

These traditions are based on 12 Steps that will help you understand alcoholism, yourself and the recovery process. The key to recovery is being able to take care of yourself physically, emotionally and spiritually. In an abusive relationship these are usually the areas that suffer injury. Al-Anon's Twelve Steps promote healing. The following are the Twelve Steps of Al-Anon:[1]

1. We admitted that we were powerless over alcohol and that our lives had become unmanageable.
2. We came to believe that a Power greater than ourselves could restore us to sanity.
3. We made a decision to turn our will and our lives over to the care of God as we understood Him.
4. We made a searching and fearless moral inventory of ourselves.
5. We admitted to God, to ourselves, and to another human being the exact nature of our wrongs.
6. We were entirely ready to have God remove all these defects of character.
7. We humbly asked Him to remove our shortcomings.
8. We made a list of all persons we had harmed and became willing to make amends to them all.

---

[1] The Twelve Steps were taken from Alcoholics Anonymous published by AA World Services, New York. Reprinted by permission.

9. We made direct amends to such people wherever possible, except when to do so would injure them or others.

10. We continued to take personal inventory and when we were wrong, promptly admitted it.

11. We sought through prayer and meditation to improve our conscious contact with God as we understood Him, praying only for knowledge of His will for us and the power to carry that out.

12. Having had a spiritual awakening as the result of these steps, we tried to carry this message to others, and to practice these principles in all our affairs.

In summary, there are several things to remember about your recovery from someone else's drinking. First, it is your recovery that must be the focus. Second, help is available to you if you will use it. Moreover, you can recover; do not allow his drinking or his excuses to control your recovery. You must, however, become involved. Help will not come by doing nothing. It will not be delivered to your mailbox. Finally, you must make a commitment to go beyond the negative effects of alcoholism in your life. The first part of this commitment is getting help for yourself. This book can only explain and offer insight into understanding and getting help. We can discuss alternatives and strategies. We can offer guidelines, support and hope. Only you can recover for yourself.

AFTERTHOUGHTS

Sorrow is so easy to express and yet so hard to tell.

—Joni Mitchell

I'm not frightened of the darkness outside. It's the darkness inside houses I don't like.

—Shelagh Delaney

It is not easy to find happiness in ourselves, and it is not possible to find it elsewhere.

—Agnes Repplier

Everybody gets so much common information all day long that they lose their common sense.

—Gertrude Stein

Nobody has ever measured, not even poets, how much a heart can hold.

—Zelda Fitzgerald

X

WHAT ABOUT THE CHILDREN?

The doctors told me I would never walk, but my mother told me I would, so I believed my mother.

—Wilma Rudolph

Families under stress produce children under stress. If you have children, they, too, are affected by abuse and alcoholism. Although you may see these abuses as primarily problems in your relationship, your children are experiencing them, too, from a different perspective.

What is the best thing that parents can give children? Love, affection, understanding and guidance are often considered to be what children need from parents. However, have you ever considered that perhaps "getting along" with each other is the best thing parents can give their children? The stress, arguing, fear and manipulation that exist in an abusive relationship affect your ability to be a healthy parent.

Spouse abuse is also a form of child abuse. Hurting someone a child loves also hurts the child. If you were raised in an abusive home, try to remember how it felt to see one of your parents abused. Remember the fear you felt not only for that parent, but also for yourself or your siblings. How did it feel to see someone you cared about abused and not able to stop it? Your children see and feel these things about you and your victimization. Still, no child wants to admit a parent is an abuser and causes pain for the family.

Many of these same feelings apply to alcoholic parents. There are certain feelings and pain that exist for the child when his or her parent is addicted to alcohol. Watching a mother try to handle a father's drinking creates many mixed feelings for children. For children who live in a family where both violence and alcohol abuse exist, the effects are multiplied.

ABUSED PARENT, ABUSED CHILD

There is solid evidence that your abusive relationship affects your children. Studies reveal that 45 percent of children whose mothers are battered are themselves physically abused (Roy 1988). This statistic does not include any abuse children may suffer at the hands of the mother. Therefore, the actual rate of abuse against children whose parents have an abusive relationship is higher. Consider, too, that the tactics abusive men use to control women are also used to control their children. Abuse in a family does not exist in a vacuum.

Not all children in an abusive family or an alcoholic family will be affected exactly alike, nor will they all identify with the same problems. However, all children in an abusive household can benefit from help in how to survive the parents' troubled relationship, and also how to handle their feelings and recover from the experience. How can you tell if, and to what extent, your own children have been affected? These are some of the characteristics of children who are caught in the "crossfire" of an abusive relationship:

- Using violence to solve problems and conflict with other children and family members
- Tending to blame themselves for things that go wrong
- Poor impulse control; inability to put off immediate gratification
- Not understanding the dynamics of violence; often assuming it is normal and occurs in all families
- Feeling isolated from peers because of embarrassment over family violence
- Not understanding personal boundaries and often violating others' boundaries
- Tending to lash out and blame others for their own problems
- Keeping family matters secret
- Blaming Mother for Father's abusive behavior; hoping that Mother will come to her or his defense and stop Father's violence
- Blaming themselves for Father's violent behavior
- Exhibiting jittery behavior—jumpy and restless, they startle easily
- Thinking of ways to beat Father when they are old enough to stand up to him
- Low self-esteem, poor image of self and little confidence
- Showing anger at everything and everybody, especially Mother
- Displaying hyperactivity or excitable behaviors
- Unaccustomed to setting limits
- Unable to recognize, label or express feelings appropriately, if at all
- Tending to be happy one minute and angry the next for no apparent reason
- Vowing to never hit a woman but ending up hitting just like the father
- Often experiencing physical, verbal or sexual abuse
- Always experiencing emotional abuse

Not all children will display all these characteristics. Some children in abusive families will develop conduct disorders and are likely to be in trouble most of the time. Other children will learn to become incredibly compliant. On the outside they will appear as if they are doing very well and are unaffected, but on the inside they are in turmoil and are afraid to express their feelings. Regardless of where your children are on the continuum, we know that they have been exposed to an abusive situation, may have been abused themselves and deeply affected by it, and will benefit from support from either you or someone outside the family.

Children from dysfunctional families are called "high risk" children. When they grow up, they are at a high risk for relationship problems, low self-esteem, abuse, chemical dependency and many other problems. They are especially prone to repeating the same abusive process they experienced as children when they have their own families. However, not all high risk children remain at a high risk. They can be helped. Those children who are left on their own to struggle with family problems in silence will remain at risk. Those children who can share the "family secret" with others or with at least one parent, who get into support groups, enjoy childhood activities and develop a healthy sense of self apart from the abuse will lower their risk of personal problems and of repeating the same behaviors in their adult lives. In order to do this, your children will need help. They need you.

Don't be afraid to admit that your children are affected. It is better to help them overcome exposure to the problems than to deny that they have been affected, thereby depriving them of intervention. Don't interpret their need as your failure to protect them. You cannot control an abusive situation. Do not accept responsibility for the way your children have been affected by his drinking or his abuse. Do not accept the blame for their problems. You are not to blame.

You are responsible, however, if you are aware that your children have been damaged by witnessing the abuse or being abused themselves and you do nothing to help them. Then you are ignoring the problem and their needs. You will be better prepared to help your children if you know how they are likely to react to and interpret abuse.

CHILDREN OF ALCOHOLICS

You may be surprised to discover that many of the feelings children of alcoholics have are the same as yours as a victim of abuse. However, one of the strongest feelings children experience is a complete sense of powerlessness. Children in alcoholic families experience three forms of powerlessness. First, they are powerless over the parent's drinking. They cannot stop the drinking and they cannot get sober for the parent. Second, they are powerless over the relationship between the parents. They cannot improve this abusive relationship. What is unfortunate about these first two forms of powerlessness is that children usually do not believe that they are powerless and they will attempt many forms of behavior in order to make things better. But things do not get better and the feelings of powerlessness increase. The third form of powerlessness occurs because children cannot leave. Unless they are removed by formal intervention, or the parent removes them, they will remain in the family—unprotected and untreated. You know what it is like to feel powerless as an adult; imagine how it must feel for your children!

Besides powerlessness, which is the primary feeling children experience, there are at least seven common areas of concern for young children of alcoholics (Morehouse 1982). Not all children will express them the same way, but one way or another most children who endure an alcohol abusing relationship feel them. As you read, try to see the issues from a child's point of view.

WORRYING ABOUT THE HEALTH OF AN ALCOHOLIC PARENT

Many young children do not understand the dynamics of alcoholism, but they know what they see. They see a person who is not well, who does not take care of himself and whose behavior is often deteriorating. Also, one of the parents may tell them, "Daddy is not feeling well today." This creates a fear of what will happen to them if something happens to the alcoholic. Another emotional dimension of your child's worrying is a fear of abandonment. Your children do not understand all the issues. They only understand that adults are supposed to be there to help. When this help is jeopardized it produces a feeling of abandonment.

FEELING ANGER AND UPSET
OVER UNPREDICTABILITY AND INCONSISTENCIES

Unfortunately, most alcoholics are highly inconsistent in fulfilling their parenting responsibilities. They can vacillate between ignoring and being abusive to the children one day and being extremely loving or supportive the next. Alcoholic parents typically display four distinct patterns in their role relationships with their children. One is when they are actually drinking. Another is when they are experiencing a hangover, feeling guilty or remorseful. The third pattern is when the alcoholic is sober and appears normal. The fourth pattern usually occurs before drinking and is marked by high levels of anxiety and agitation.

The nonalcoholic parent is usually so busy trying to cope with the alcoholism and her relationship with the spouse that the children feel ignored. They believe that Mother has no time for them, that they are not as important as the drinking, and they do not understand why their nonalcoholic parent does not support them.

WORRYING ABOUT FIGHTS AND ARGUMENTS BETWEEN PARENTS

Many years ago Margaret Cork, a researcher on children, found that 95 percent of young children of alcoholics considered the arguing and fighting between their parents as a greater problem for them than the drinking (Cork 1969). This attitude does not change and is carried into adulthood. In a later study it was found that adult children of alcoholics ranked getting their parents to get along better with each other as a higher priority than getting the alcoholic parent into treatment (Ackerman 1993). As mentioned earlier, not only do the children see this as the number one problem, but they often blame themselves for it. It is common for a child to spend a tremendous amount of energy trying to help parents get along better. Then, too, many children believe that the reason the parent drinks or argues is somehow their fault. Children do not cause alcoholism in their parents. Children do not cause parents to abuse each other. Children are caught in the middle.

BEING SCARED AND UPSET BY VIOLENCE OR THE THREAT OF VIOLENCE

Your children know that there is some connection between the drinking and the violence. They do not know exactly what the connection is, but they do know that the two often occur together. They live in fear, wondering when the next drinking bout will occur and if it will be followed by violence.

BEING UPSET BY A PARENT'S DEVIANT BEHAVIOR

Not only is the *drinking* upsetting for the children; they fear the *behaviors* often associated with the drinking as much or more. Those behaviors that get the parent in trouble, embarrass the child, involve the child or must be covered up by the child can be devastating. Children do not like to admit that their parent is causing problems for them or anyone else. It is not uncommon to find many young children in alcohol abusing families suffering from stress-related illnesses.

BEING DISAPPOINTED BY BROKEN PROMISES AND FEELING UNLOVED

"If you loved us, you would stop" is a statement often heard from children of alcoholic or abusive parents. Since the alcoholic parent doesn't stop, the children think, "I guess this means that we're not loved." Children also think, "If you loved me, you wouldn't do such things." Thus the child feels unloved. On the other hand, since many children believe it is something about them that causes the parent to drink, they believe they are unworthy of love. They believe it is their own fault they receive no love.

Breaking promises to children in the alcoholic family becomes a norm. No matter how often it happens, it brings disappointment. Usually these broken promises are followed by even more grandiose promises, which will only be broken later.

FEELING RESPONSIBLE FOR THEIR PARENT'S DRINKING

"If I were better, he wouldn't drink so much" is a statement that has been repeated by many children in treatment for their parent's drinking. Children see things from their own point of view and believe that they cause events. They believe it is something about them that influences the drinking. We are sure that you can identify with this feeling. If you have ever blamed yourself for the abuse in your relationship, you have held yourself responsible for causing it. Even though children do not actually cause parents to drink, this does not mean that they understand or believe it.

HOW YOU CAN HELP

Just as you have your own ideas, beliefs, responses, feelings and fears about your relationship, so do your children. You see your life from your point of view and your children see it from theirs. However, one major difference exists between you and your children. You are an adult and can choose to go for help on your own. Your children can't find help by themselves and will need you to support their efforts. Do not wait for the alcoholic to get help before you help your children. It may be too late. Unfortunately, most alcoholics do not get sober. Do not wait for the abuse to stop or until you leave him before you get help for the children, either. At least 50 percent of abused women who leave a relationship return to it with their children.

Your children will need help in at least one of three areas, and perhaps all three, depending upon their circumstances. The three areas are: needing support for the abuse that they have witnessed; being exposed to the alcohol abuse of your spouse or yourself; and being the victims themselves of physical or sexual abuse. The following suggestions are offered to help you help your children (Ackerman 1987). Remember, they cannot do it by themselves. They need you.

Be flexible regarding the demands that you make on yourself and your children, remembering that difficult situations call for adaptable measures.

From repeated attempts to control the situation, the alcoholic home often becomes a rigid family system. However, too much control over our children may be interpreted by them as blaming them. Remember, they did not cause the alcoholism; they are only trying to survive it.

Try not to isolate yourself and your family from outside interaction or from interaction within your home.

Realizing that you want to protect and help your children, you can try to insulate them from negative reactions to alcoholism, but do not isolate them. Isolation and feelings of uniqueness are two of the stronger feelings for most children of alcoholics. Do not magnify these feelings by keeping them isolated. They will need external supports to help withstand internal conflicts.

Do not blame your children for wanting to get help.

Often, parents in the alcoholic home are embarrassed when their children are being helped. This is your embarrassment, not theirs. Do not be offended that they have turned to someone else. Professional help is necessary in serious circumstances. This is even more true if your children are being physically or sexually abused. They will need outside help. Do not blame them for wanting to stop an abusive situation. You do not want to be blamed for trying to stop yours either.

The alcoholic is not to be excused from parenting.

It is important for the children that the alcoholic parent is still as much a positive part of the family as possible. Remember that the alcoholic is still a role model for the children and will teach them many other behaviors besides alcoholism. One of these will be the modeling of good parenting. All children need love, concern, acceptance and guidance; being alcoholic does not excuse parents from providing these to their children. Do not excuse them from responsibilities. It only makes it easier to drink, while they continue to neglect the children.

Avoid pressuring your children, either verbally or indirectly through your actions, to take sides in conflicts you have with your spouse.

Your children do not need, nor do they usually want, to take sides. Instead, they want you, their parents, to behave in ways that do not demand their siding with one or the other. If they are forced into taking a parent's side, they will face even more problems. Furthermore, pressure on children to take sides in marital conflicts usually intensifies the conflict for everyone.

Avoid using the opinions of your children about the use of alcohol or the alcoholic parent to get at the alcoholic.

Using your children against your spouse is like taking sides. It places them in a vulnerable position between you and your spouse. Your children may even become a target for the abusive spouse who believes the children have talked negatively about him or have turned against him. It may also cause your child to refrain from sharing feelings with you.

When home life is excessively disruptive or verbally abusive and your children go off to be alone, seek them out and comfort them.

During family drinking episodes or episodes of violence, many children hide in the bathroom or in their rooms because of fear or frustration. These episodes can be very upsetting. You should try to avoid letting your children go to sleep upset. When there is conflict and disruption, talk with them at the first opportunity. Try a hug. It will go a long way to calming their internal conflict and will reinforce that they are not alone.

Avoid placing your oldest child in the position of being a confidant or surrogate parent.

Making a surrogate parent of your children places too much strain on them and may also anger your spouse, whose role they are being asked to fill. Children who are put into the confidant role often suffer from "emotional incest." This occurs when the parent shares information with the child that should be shared only with the spouse. Also, when parents whose place they are taking resume their duties, the children must revert to their original position in the family. This shifting of roles can lead your children to have feelings of inconsistency and to experience serious personal problems.

Encourage and support your children becoming involved in school and community activities.

Your children need opportunities to develop relationships with others in activities outside your home. Activities outside the home may help your children understand that they can accomplish things and can be independent of undesirable influences in your home. All children under stress need an "emotional oasis." Outside experiences can provide an emotional rest.

Try to arrange times for your children to have their friends visit regularly.

Your home should also be their home. Some alcoholics drink in patterns and provide some opportunity for quiet family conditions. However, if your children have friends over and the alcoholic parent is drinking, do not further embarrass them or the friends by confronting the alcoholic in front of them. The time to talk with an alcoholic about drinking is not when the drinking is taking place.

Avoid exacting promises from your children that they will never drink.

If children of alcoholics decide to drink later in life, this promise may cause unneeded guilt. It will also imply to them that they cannot handle alcohol. Many alcoholics have high levels of guilt about their drinking. Guilt may even increase their level of drinking because of a perceived inability, often learned in the home, to control alcohol consumption. However, there is nothing wrong with letting your children know about the problems of excessive drinking or about the risk they face of developing alcohol problems because of having an alcoholic parent.

Avoid constantly asking your children if you should leave your spouse.

Unless separation has been decided upon, in which case the children should be consulted, questioning your children about when or if you should leave your spouse only adds to the children's confusion over why you remain together. This question is particularly inappropriate for small children. They feel that parents are supposed to be responsible, and here a parent is asking a young child the most difficult of questions. Also, should you not separate once you have raised these questions, your children may live in fear of a separation from then on. This adds to your marital difficulties and to the personal problems of your children.

Educate yourself about alcoholism and community resources.

It is difficult to help yourself or others unless you know what you are dealing with. Much frustration in alcoholic families arises from fears of the unknown effects of drinking. Although you may not be able to get your spouse to stop drinking, you can better prepare yourself and your children for survival.

Become involved in community resources or self-help groups for family members of alcoholics.

There are many support groups available for all ages of children of alcoholics. Enroll your children in these groups and support their attendance. There are many family programs in which you can become involved, with or without the alcoholic or abusive parent. You and your children can go to these programs together.

If your alcoholic spouse seeks help, try to become involved as a family in the treatment process.

Alcoholism affects the entire family, and all members will benefit from help. Assuming that the family remains together, allowing the alcoholic to enter treatment alone is to deny family support for sobriety and, more important, is to deny help for yourself and your children. Family members learn to adapt to the recovering alcoholic. If the alcoholic quits drinking, family life can change. The family, which of course includes your children, must be prepared to accept the alcoholic member back into the family physically and emotionally. Total recovery from alcoholism may require a total family effort. Remember, however, to keep the focus on your children and yourself.

Do not dwell on the past; learn from it.

Whether or not sobriety occurs, do not allow yourself to fall into the "what I could have done" syndrome. What you can do now is more important for your children. Their past is not as long as their future. Help your children by not making yesterday "eternal." To do so will always not only affect tomorrow, but will affect tomorrow negatively. Children often recover faster than adults. Do not impede their progress by dwelling on the past.

Use alternative and new endeavors, not old habits.

Change will be needed if you want your life and the lives of your children to improve. This means exploring alternatives and investing energy. This will be difficult because of the lack of energy in the alcoholic home, but the family will not get better by repeating negative behaviors, nor will it get better by doing nothing. Active alternatives are needed.

Stop doing what you do not do.

Break your negative habits. For example, you do not discuss alcoholism; you do not discuss the abuse; you do not go for help; you do not try alternatives; you do not feel that anything will help; and you do not recover. These habits become built-in obstacles or excuses to avoid recovery. You can stop negative inactivity through positive actions.

Take care of yourself.

It will be easier and more realistic for you to help your children if you feel better about yourself. Your children need physically and emotionally healthy parents.

Get help now!

Don't wait for the right time. It has arrived. Many people believe they will do something about their lives when the time is right. Right for what? Postponing help only allows the problems to continue. Your children need you to act now. If you are concerned about protecting and helping your children, get help for them now. Do not deny their needs because you are not sure of yours.

AFTERTHOUGHTS

If you cannot trust your father and mother to love you and accept you and protect you, then you are an orphan, although your parents are upstairs asleep in their bed.

—Elizabeth Feur

The events of childhood do not pass, but repeat themselves like seasons of the year.

—Eleanor Farjeon

Words are more powerful than perhaps anyone suspects, and once daily engraved in a child's mind, they are not easily eradicated.

—May Sarton

I don't think of all the misery, but of all the beauty that still remains.

—Anne Frank

We must not, in trying to think about how we can make a big difference, ignore the small daily differences we can make which, over time, add up to big differences that we often cannot foresee.

—Marian Wright Edleman

XI

WHAT TO EXPECT IF HE GOES FOR HELP

❦

Love yourself first and everything else falls into line. You really have to love yourself to get anything done in this world.

—Lucille Ball

Even though he may go for help, the focus of this chapter is still the same as all the other chapters. We are concerned about you. What does it mean if he goes for help? What kind of help will he receive? Should you support him or not, and how will all of this affect you? Learning what to expect when he goes for help is important, considering that most abused women either stay with the man or return to him. When he goes for help, be sensitive to several things.

• He is going for help because he needs help for his own behavior, something that you did not cause.

- Do not expect instant results, such as no more drinking or no more abuse. Protect yourself.
- Do not support or accept any explanation for his quitting once he begins.
- Do not believe in magical cures. Healthy results take time, energy, commitment and involvement in bona fide treatment programs.
- Be prepared for relapse and make appropriate plans now. Do not accept any blame for his relapse.
- If he is both drinking and abusive, do not expect both to stop if he seeks help for only one.
- Do not believe that if he seeks help you do not need your own recovery program.

Why do you need to know what is involved when a man seeks help for his abusiveness? First, you will be better prepared to respond effectively to your needs and to his if you are aware of what he is doing. Second, many women want to save their relationships and they welcome his treatment. Third, you may want to support his change and understand how to be a healthy supporter without accepting unnecessary blame.

WHAT DOES HE DO?

There are no clear-cut steps to becoming non-abusive, and no treatment model that guarantees success. However, there are some processes or growth stages along the way toward stopping the abuse. They do not all happen at once or necessarily in the order stated here. But if they occur, the chances of stopping the abusive behavior are improved. Since there are so many similarities between alcohol abuse and spouse abuse patterns for the male, many of these stages apply to some extent to both. The most prominent growth stages include:

- Asking for help
- Breaking through denial

- Owning the abusive behavior and accepting responsibility
- Understanding the consequences of abusive behavior
- Learning what emotions start the abusive behavior
- Learning alternatives to replace the abusive behavior

The first stage of the change process involves asking for help. Whether he asks for help because he wants you back, feels something is wrong or has legal problems does not matter now. What is essential is that he reaches out. Confirm his plea and agree that he does need help. This is not the time to second-guess whether he has a problem or not. Do not let him "off the hook" because he has finally admitted to the problem and you begin to feel sorry for him. Just as the responses of others to an abused woman influence what she may do and how she feels about herself, people's responses to a man's questioning of himself and his need for help will influence his actions. These messages confirm that he needs help. Do not change the message now.

If he talks only to other untreated men like himself, he will gain no insights into his abusive behaviors. Other men who accept and practice abuse are not going to tell him he has a problem. Therefore, family members, friends, clergy and professionals can do him a great service by confirming to him that he needs help.

Whatever the source of the message that he receives when he asks for help, the message must be consistent. The courts could mandate counseling for a man who is arrested for assaulting his wife or has a PFA issued against him. Parole officers can request treatment for any of their male clients who are abusive. The abused spouses can make a stipulation that he must attend an abuser's program before considering reconciliation. These are a few of the possibilities that can motivate a man towards getting help. The saying, "You can lead a horse to water, but you can't make him drink" applies if you try to force someone to get help. However, you can lead a horse to water and see if he's thirsty!

While you may assist him in finding resources for his problem, don't take responsiblity for making all the arrangements for him. He must ask for help and do the things that are necessary to obtain it. When you attend to these details for him, he is doing nothing for himself. If the help he receives is ineffective, this is one more thing he can blame on you. Be sure to establish your own boundaries in terms of what you expect once he admits he needs help. By knowing where you stand, it will be easier for you to make the correct decisions for yourself while he is getting help.

BREAKING THROUGH DENIAL

Denial can be as strong for abusive men as for alcoholics. If both problems are evident, which is more often the case than not, each is intensified by the other. Spouse abuse and alcohol abuse do not cause each other, but they are frequently partners. The chances of recognizing either problem is better if the denial is broken.

The chances are greater for the alcohol problem being recognized first. There are many treatment centers for alcohol and drug abuse, plus publicity, advertising and public awareness of these problems. Insurance companies may sponsor treatment for alcoholism as part of an employees' health benefit package. But these health benefits are unlikely to extend to spouse abuse. The public is just becoming aware of domestic violence as a societal problem, and there is even less awareness of treatment programs.

Denial in an abusive relationship is an inability to recognize and face the reality of having abused someone. It is an inability to see her pain and terror, or to recognize the way the violence has affected her and everyone else in the family. This denial is reinforced by society's acceptance of abusive behavior. Denial can protect us from looking at ourselves and from seeing things we don't want to recognize in ourselves. The stereotype of a man needing to be in control, in charge of the situation and strong, is one that must be refuted in order to break through the denial.

A new way of treating male abusers that is proving to be somewhat effective is having them participate in a group of males who are also abusive to their wives. A group can help him confront his denial because he is surrounded by others who are like himself. He is not alone, his isolation is broken, his secret is out and other members will not let him get away with denying his abusive behavior.

A group can be the most effective way to deal with abusers. Men can help each other change instead of reinforcing abusive behavior. This concept is similar to AA, where alcoholics meet with other alcoholics; seeing others succeed gives hope to those trying to change. Both of these groups are dependent upon the individual breaking through denial.

If he turns to you and asks, "Do I really have a drinking problem?" or "Am I really that abusive?" what will you say? We hope that you will look him straight in the eye and say, "Read my lips. YES!"

ACCEPTING RESPONSIBILITY

Once denial is broken through, he can begin to look at his own behavior, admit to and accept it. Talking about some of his actions and admitting he behaved abusively helps him to own the behaviors. Giving up the notion that, "She caused me to hit her" or "She nagged until I couldn't stand it any longer" is all part of his taking responsibility for the behavior. Recognizing what he did and realizing no one else "caused" him to do it involves accepting the behavior as his own. Owning the abusive behavior is essential to stopping it. Once a man recognizes that he is responsible for his actions, he can begin to take steps to help himself and reshape his behavior.

While it is important that he hold himself accountable for his behaviors, he must not own the treatment. He must accept that he cannot treat himself, but that there are others who can assist him. If he thinks that he needs no one but himself to change, he is more likely to relapse. Owning the behavior and owning the solution are two different things.

Just because he admits that he owns the abusive behavior does not mean that he will stop. This is only part of the process. However, some men will stop here and use ownership as a rationalization for abuse. Someone who does this makes statements like, "That's right, I'm no good," "It's all my fault" and "What do you expect? I can't help myself?" Do not accept these rationalizations. Reinforce that with ownership comes the responsibility to change. Otherwise you will "disown" the relationship and move out.

UNDERSTANDING THE CONSEQUENCES

The consequences of abusive behavior are arrest, jail, loss of friends, loss of self-control, losing the very person he wants so desperately to keep and control, scaring his children, not getting close to the ones he loves, alienating friends, losing support from his family and receiving pity or fear from others. In treatment he will learn that actions produce reactions, and that his abusive behaviors have negative consequences not only for himself, but for others as well.

He will learn that many of his actions towards you, some that he didn't recognize as such, are abusive. What he considers normal relationship expectations and behaviors will be clarified and reinterpreted as being abnormal. His image of how males should respond to women and children will be challenged. And, depending on what got him into treatment, he will come face to face with being held accountable for his "normal" behavior.

Learning What Emotions Start Abuse

Abusive spouses have reported that anything can set them off: a late dinner, being late from grocery shopping, not silencing a crying child or talking to other men. Abusive men have a difficult time naming the exact reason they became violent. They may have had a tough day at work and were chastised by the boss, thus feeling frustrated, angry, resentful, weak or inadequate. These are all feelings that seem to be channeled into the one emotion abusive men consistently are able to recognize: anger.

Recognizing what he is feeling and knowing what each feeling entails can help him begin to change his behavior. Understanding what his fears are, what expectations he has of himself and others and what values he has can help control the emotions behind his negative behaviors. Understanding these feelings, fears and expectations as cues to negative behavior can help him recognize those times when he may become abusive. Recognizing the source of his feelings as something other than simply anger sensitizes him to the behavior that follows. If he can acknowledge the many feelings inside—where they come from and why he has them—he can start to learn how to deal with them appropriately.

LEARNING ALTERNATIVES TO ABUSE

The more alternatives to abuse or drinking that abusive people become aware of, the higher the probability that they will realize they do have choices. Most abusive men are very rigid in certain aspects of their lives. Stopping abusive behavior requires flexibility, not rigidity. It requires recognizing new behaviors and using them. A good treatment program will reinforce that a man can stop drinking and stop being abusive. He does have choices other than hitting his wife and getting drunk.

One of the best alternatives we hope that abusive men discover is that instead of drinking or being abusive, they can go to meetings and get help, whether it is AA, an abusive men's group or both. Continuing the abuse is unacceptable. Any telephone book in the country will put him in touch with Alcoholics Anonymous. There are about 150 programs throughout the country that offer help specifically to abusive men. For a listing of these programs he can write for the Ending Men's Violence National Referral Directory to RAVEN, P.O. Box 24159, St. Louis, MO 63130.

A group tends to break the isolation and provide a support network. A "buddy system" develops whereby abusers can call each other for support. He is not alone and can talk with others who have progressed beyond him and who are proof that change is possible. Other members can confront each other concerning the seriousness of their behavior and its consequences. When a man realizes that the positive results he sees in those around him are also available to him, he begins to recognize that he and his family do not have to live like this. However, merely seeing the alternatives is not enough. He has to demonstrate and live the changes.

WHEN HELPING HIM HURTS YOU

What is your role if he goes for help? If you still love him, want to stay in the relationship or reunite, you may choose to support him. Other women have long since detached from their abuse partners and are no longer concerned about what they do. However, for those of you who remain attached for one reason or another, it is important that you be very clear and honest with yourself about helping him and how much you should help.

How do you know if you are doing too much for him? A good indicator would be if you feel that helping him is hurting you. If, by helping, all the same old patterns of control, blame, arguments, violence, excessive drinking, loss of your self-esteem, poor communication and threats remain, then you are again sacrificing yourself for him. The idea of recovery, if you stay with him, is for both of you, not just him. It should offer an opportunity to change and to feel good about yourselves.

AFTERTHOUGHTS

Marriage . . . cannot . . . offer emotional security, for such security is the achievement of the individual.

—Germaine Greer

You lose a lot of time hating people.

—Marian Anderson

Genuine forgiveness does not deny anger but faces it head-on.

—Alice Miller

You have to have confidence in your ability, and then be tough enough to follow through.

—Rosalynn Carter

The best protector any woman can have . . . is courage.

—Elizabeth Cady Stanton

XII

RECOVERY:
HOW DO YOU KNOW WHEN
YOU'RE GETTING BETTER?

I do not want to die until I have faithfully made the most of my talent and cultivated the seed that was placed in me until the last small twig has grown.

—Kathe Kollwitz

THE CIRCUS

Once there was a little girl who had never been to the circus and she heard that one was coming to her town. Excitement, anticipation and joy filled her for days while she waited. She knew the circus was coming because she saw a sign on a telephone pole. It would cost $3.00 to see it. The little girl saved her money so that she would be ready when it arrived. Finally, the day came when the circus train arrived and a great parade marched through the middle of town. The little girl went to Main Street early so that she could find a place on the curb and be up front; she did not want to miss anything. She watched as the parade began far down the street, becoming more and more excited as it drew closer to her. She marveled at the elephants, lions in cages, bears, seals and other circus animals as they passed by her. It was everything she thought it would be. And finally the clowns came by. She laughed and loved everything they did. When the last clown passed, the parade was over. She had seen the circus and was very pleased. She went up to the last clown and handed him her $3.00, then she went home with her memories of the day safe in her heart. A few days later, she heard her friends at school talking about the circus, but they described it differently from how she had experienced it. They had been to the circus under the tent and had watched all the acts in the three rings. The little girl realized that she had missed the actual circus, but tried to comfort herself by telling herself that she saw the parade. However, she did feel that she had missed something. She had missed the main event.

YOUR RECOVERY

When it comes to your recovery, you are the main event. If he decides to go for help, he is working on his recovery, not yours. He cannot recover for you, and you cannot recover for him. If your relationship starts to get a little better and your hopes begin to rise, don't confuse this with personal recovery. Whether he receives help or not, or whether you stay in the relationship or not, recovery is your right. Don't let him persuade you that there is no need for you to take care of yourself.

Recovery is something new to you, and therefore unknown. Just like the little girl, whose unfamiliarity with what a circus was cost her the chance to actually see one, you are unfamiliar with recovery. Do not be afraid to want all there is in recovery. It will be both exciting for you and intimidating, but it can never be as intimidating as your abusive relationship. In recovery you will grow. We are sure that you will feel growing pains, but these pains are never as agonizing as the ones that you have already endured. Your recovery is your path to improving the quality of your life.

Two themes have dominated this book. One is often heard in the stories shared by abused women: self-blame, despair, feeling used and being without hope. The other is recovery. Which of these themes will you choose for yourself?

Too often the idea of helping the victimized woman is merely to ensure her survival. But survival alone is not enough. Your recovery from the experience, your right to improve the quality of your life physically, emotionally and spiritually, and your right to become and live as the person you would like to be are far more important. Have you really survived something if it has taken important parts of you away?

Recovery is not only going back and working through your past, it is also going forward. We have attempted to reveal the challenges you will face, the issues and feelings that must be considered, the tactics for helping yourself and the processes of recovery from an abusive relationship. You are now at the point of applying these ideas to your life or remaining where you are. Only you can make these decisions. You do have a choice. We hope that you have raised your expectations, not only of other people, but also of yourself and your life.

WHAT IS RECOVERY?

Recovery is freedom.

You become free from the past, free to choose your future, free to enjoy your life and free to feel good about yourself.

Recovery is a journey.

Recovery is a continuing process. It means you are growing to your full potential. It is never a destination. There are no limits in recovery; only those that you impose can stop you.

Recovery requires change.

You cannot recover by doing nothing. Many of us fear change because we don't know the final outcome. However, what we probably fear the most about change is its direction and rate. If a change is about to occur in your life and it is contrary to what you want, it can be very stressful. If a change you desire occurs too slowly or too quickly for you to adjust to it, it can also be upsetting. If you can adjust to the rate of the change and it is moving you in the direction you prefer, it will not cause you stress. Remember these two things when contemplating your recovery. If you take it a little at a time you will be happier in recovery. No one said that you had to recover perfectly and all at once.

Recovery is repetition.

Children teach us that often the quality of life is measured in repetitions. You can enjoy spending time with a child while playing a game, going to the zoo or just being together, and the child will say, "Let's do it again." Recovery, therefore, should be called "recovering." You do not have to stop at any given place. Find comfort in knowing that you can become as healthy as you can be today, knowing that tomorrow you have the privilege of doing it again.

Recovery is one day at a time.

You do not have to recover all at once. You have been abused or exposed to an abusive relationship for a long time. It will take time to heal and then to grow. The important thing is not how far you have gone, but that you are on your way.

Recovery is yours.

Others cannot recover for you, and once begun, no one can take it away. Recovering people do not allow others to take their inner peace away. This does not mean that there will not be other struggles or painful days, but rather that you have developed an inner peace and you know how to use it to protect yourself.

Recovery is joy.

We agree that there is no joy in being abused, but there is joy when you find a way to stop it, and find a way to help yourself. When you begin to live your life with meaning and happiness, you will experience joy.

Recovery is a gift that you give yourself.

The key to recovery is inside you. We all know the story of the person who is walking down the street and notices a neighbor looking in the front yard for something that is lost. The person stops and asks, "What are you looking for?" "Lost my keys," the neighbor replies; and so the person helps look for the lost keys in the front yard. After awhile the person asks, "Just where do you think that you lost them?" "I know exactly where I lost them; I lost them in the house," the neighbor responds. "Why are we looking out here then?" the person asks. "Because there's more light out here!"

The keys are in the house. Recovery is inside you, but it can be facilitated by others. Many people and groups will help you, as we have stated and have encouraged you to try throughout this book. You hold the keys to unlocking the door to recovery. You can unlock the door and go inside.

The method of recovery you choose is up to you. We only ask that you choose one and begin your journey. Remember that you have suffered alone, but that you can recover with the help of others. Recovery will not be something that you do, but a process and meetings you attend; you will experience it in the way you live. If you are recovering, your life will improve . . . but how do you know if you are getting better?

HOW TO TELL WHEN YOU ARE GETTING BETTER

If you have tried many of the ideas in this book and wonder if you are getting better, ask yourself this basic question: "If someone accused me of recovering, could they find enough evidence to convict me?" Not all abused women will take the same paths to recovery. Not all will need to take as long as others. Not all will arrive at the same place. However, there is always the difference between saying that you are recovering and living the recovery. Which of your behaviors suggest you are recovering? The following will not apply to everyone, but we are sure you now know which ones describe you. Read each one, assess where you are and keep trying if it is not yet part of your recovery. Remember that your recovery is a process and that you will be growing by degrees. The idea is to keep getting better.

You Know You Are Getting Better When You Can Celebrate Yourself and Your Survival

You are a survivor and you should learn to appreciate yourself. Imagine that you are in a group of people who are lost in the Arctic. You and your group have managed to survive without the help of others for many months in the cold. Finally, you are discovered and rescued. Wouldn't you celebrate? Wouldn't you acknowledge the strengths that enabled you to endure? If you are still reading this book, it is not your weaknesses that have brought you this far, but your strengths. The strengths that have allowed you to endure will also be the strengths that will help you to recover.

You No Longer Live in Fear

You have done something to bring about changes in your life and are no longer living in fear of abuse. However this has come about, you believe that you can protect yourself and that you will not return to your previous abusive situation. This part of your recovery tells you that even if you are in the same relationship, you will no longer tolerate being abused. You have set guidelines for yourself and you stick to them. You have not only protected yourself from abuse, but you no longer fear the unknown, a fear that previously kept you from getting help.

YOU RESPECT YOURSELF

With recovery comes respecting and accepting yourself, both your positive and negative behaviors. It also includes a commitment to take better care of yourself and not allow others to abuse you. When you respect yourself, you elevate your opinion of yourself to the level where you realize that you are a person worthy of respect. You believe that you have rights, dignity and assets. You are taking care of yourself physically, emotionally and spiritually out of respect for the person that you have become.

YOU HAVE WORKED THROUGH YOUR GRIEF

In recovery from any abusive experience there is always a process of grieving over what has happened to you. When you have honestly worked through your grief, you are no longer depressed and are capable of going beyond the hurt. If we are hurt, we not only grieve the injury, but we also grieve what we have missed because of the injury. Much of your pain is not only a direct result of the abusive nature of your relationship, but also an indirect result of realizing what you have missed. If you are in an unhealthy relationship, then you have missed being in a healthy one. You may have missed out on joyous times, feeling good about yourself, knowing what it means to care for someone and having that person care for you, and living your life the way that you would like. When you begin to control the grieving process, when it no longer controls you, you know that you are getting better.

YOU CAN HANDLE YOUR MEMORIES

The idea is not to erase your memories, but to be able to handle them. If you have survived living your past you can survive remembering it, particularly if you do not have to remember alone. You know that you are getting better because you do not live in fear of what is in your own mind. When you can handle your memories, you know that you are no longer minimizing or rationalizing what has happened. We all have emotional flashbacks to unpleasant memories. When you feel one coming on, take the appropriate steps to help yourself. The recovering person recovers not only from the physical situation, but also from the memories that have accompanied it.

YOU CAN TRUST

After years of betrayal it is difficult to trust anyone. Also, it becomes difficult to trust your own instincts and decisions. When you begin to trust that you know what is best for you because of a sound recovery process, you are learning how to trust in yourself. No longer are you subjected to other people telling you what is best for you. Lack of trust will undermine any relationship.

The most difficult type of trust is trusting others with information about yourself and hoping that they will not use this information against you later. An indicator of how well you have begun to trust people and yourself is feeling comfortable sharing information about yourself that you previously kept inside. Don't be afraid to develop trust. It will allow you to fully express yourself and to share with others. Above all, you will learn to trust your feelings. When this happens, you are getting in touch with the real you. Don't be afraid to trust your feelings; they will not betray you.

YOU CAN AFFIRM YOURSELF

I can survive. I can grow and recover. I can love and be loved. I can accomplish many things. I am a good person. These are all affirmations of the kind of person that you are. When you affirm yourself, you have realized that you actually possess good qualities. You are overcoming the many negative things that you have heard about yourself from your abusive partner, and that you allowed yourself to believe. When you stop believing these erroneous messages and start believing in yourself, you are affirming your worth as a person in your own eyes.

YOU NO LONGER ARE CONTROLLED OR CONTROLLING

Recovery means that you begin to feel in control of your life again. It means that someone else is not controlling your thoughts and actions. On the other hand, it is ironic that many abused women who are controlled respond by trying to be in total control of everything around them. It is a common belief that if you control the things that upset him, then he will not lose control. The entire time you are attempting to exercise your control, you are being controlled. Being in control in an abusive situation is an illusion. If you really were in control you would have changed the situation years ago.

As you are recovering, you will notice that there are usually three areas of control that you begin to relinquish. One is that you will no longer feel you must control situations, particularly chaotic ones. It will occur to you that you do not have to be in charge all the time. Another is that you no longer feel the need to control relationships either directly or indirectly. You begin to understand that a controlling relationship is not a healthy relationship. The third type of control you relinquish is maintaining total control over your emotions as a way to protect yourself. It is ironic that once you give up all these forms of control, you begin to feel more in control of your life.

YOU CAN FEEL AGAIN

When you were not recovering, you probably experienced "compassion fatigue." This can occur when, through a lack of energy, you can no longer express or identify your feelings. You know that you would like to care and to be able to feel, but the only thing that you are feeling is emotional numbness. You may have believed a benefit of this emotional numbness was that since you no longer felt so much, you could not be hurt so deeply. By withdrawing your emotions you may have protected yourself, but in order to fully recover you will need to be able to feel your emotions and know what you are feeling.

An indicator of overcoming compassion fatigue is when you begin to separate from situations that are too emotionally draining. You become aware of not wanting to expend your emotions and energy on negative situations, so that you might use that energy for positive emotional intimacy. You will rediscover many of the positive emotions you once had that were subdued because of your abusive relationship. They will be like old friends you have not seen for a long time coming to visit. Your heart will be glad, knowing that you have not lost your ability to feel. When you start feeling joy, happiness, love and contentment, you will know that you are truly learning to feel again and that your compassion fatigue has been replaced by positive emotional energy.

YOU CAN SAY NO

When you learn to say no, you are learning that you do not have to be responsible for everything. One of the best indicators of a healthy relationship is that either party can tell the other "No" and not feel guilty. Most women in an abusive relationship indicate that they constantly feel overwhelmed by all that they have to do or that is expected of them. Part of your recovery is learning that you have choices and that you can set your own limits. You have a right to say no to demands on your time, to limit the things that you want to be responsible for, to say no to sex, to say no to abuse and to say no when you usually said yes and didn't mean it. While you are learning to say no when necessary, you are also learning to say "yes" to yourself.

YOU CAN RECEIVE

We never worry about your ability to give at this point. The true measure of recovery is your ability to receive not only what recovery has to offer, but also those things you have pursued so diligently. Imagine how painful it would be to want a loving relationship, to have people like you and love you, only to come face-to-face with exactly those things you have always wanted and to realize you have forgotten to prepare yourself to accept them. When you can accept what others positively offer you, your recovery is beginning. Recovery itself is something that you must be able to receive in order to experience it. Every time you allow yourself to receive the good that can happen to you, you grow.

For example, a small indicator of your ability to receive is being able to accept a compliment from another. Do you accept it, or discount it? If someone tells you that you look nice, do you accept it or tell them that your clothes were on sale, were a gift or are old? Do you merely return the compliment by telling them something nice about them, or do you accept it and say, "Thank you?" Remember, the nicest compliment that someone can give you is, "I love you." The next time someone says "I love you," say, "Thank you." The person may be surprised, but you won't be because you know that you are allowing yourself to grow. When you can accept another's love, and honestly believe you are worthy of that love, you are establishing and expanding your ability to receive: you are recovering.

YOU CAN EMBRACE THE SPIRIT OF RECOVERY

It is not recovery per se, or the process of recovery that tells you if you are getting better. It is the "spirit" of recovery; allowing it to grow in you indicates that you are getting better. The greatest crime in an abusive relationship occurs when a person's spirit is crushed. We do not mean your religious spirit, but rather, the human spirit in everyone that not only makes us feel alive, but makes us want to be alive. It is that part of us that gives us energy, excitement, hope and self-confidence. Recovery is searching for your human spirit and finding it. It is that inner core in you that makes you unique, while still allowing you to identify with others. What joy there is when you begin to discover that the part of you that you thought was lost or taken from you is beginning to return. It is as if you begin to find yourself. It is your human spirit that lifts you up. You will feel it, embrace it and never allow it to be taken from you again.

YOU CAN FORGIVE

Forgiveness is a quality that comes from within. Therefore, we do not expect you to unequivocally forgive all the people who have harmed you. You may choose to forgive some people for some of the things they have done, but the choice is yours. The importance of forgiveness in recovery is revealed when you know inside that you have not forgiven and that it is keeping you from recovering. Therefore, it becomes important for you to learn an inner process of forgiveness. This often requires us to accept the fact that we were harmed, and more important, that we were treated unfairly. It requires us to determine if we need to forgive and to identify how forgiveness will contribute to our recovery. Also, when trying to find forgiveness, we often need to forgive ourselves for not taking better care of ourselves or for wrongly blaming ourselves for what has happened to us.

Some people become stuck in their recovery process and don't know why. Usually, it is because not forgiving is holding them back. Again, we do not expect you to forgive everything. Some things are unforgivable now, but we can work on them and hope that some day we may find forgiveness in our hearts. Forgiving does not mean forgetting. Our memories will always be with us, but our memories become less painful as we learn to forgive. Forgiveness is not for the other person's benefit; it is for your recovery.

YOU CAN LIKE AND LOVE YOURSELF

As painful as an abusive relationship is, it is more painful to live with yourself if you do not like who you are. An abusive relationship destroys your self-concept. We begin to believe things about ourselves that make us dislike who we are. You know that you are recovering when you begin to like the person you are becoming. It is unrealistic for us to expect other people to like and love us when we do not even like ourselves.

True intimacy begins with yourself. You need to be able to have a healthy feeling of love for who you are if you expect to develop healthy intimate behaviors. When you begin to like and love yourself, you will be capable of sharing a fine person with someone else, and you will be recovering.

In summary, we hope you will develop all of these behaviors in recovery. They will not all happen at once; they will take time to develop, but they can happen. You are worth the time. You are worth your efforts and the efforts of those who will help you. You arc worthy of recovery. We wish you this journey. We wish you what we have learned, which is that no matter where we have been there is beauty, love, peace and joy inside each and every one of us, just waiting like a flower in the spring to blossom.

AFTERTHOUGHTS

What you have become is what counts.

—Liz Smith

Love as if you liked yourself, and it may happen.

—Marge Piercy

*In the bigger scheme of things the universe is not asking us to do something,
the universe is asking us to be something. And that's
a whole different thing.*

—Lucille Clifton

*Begin somewhere; you cannot build a reputation
on what you intend to do.*

—Liz Smith

Yesterday I dared to struggle. Today I dare to win.

—Bernadette Devlin

─── Resources for Help ───

IF IN IMMEDIATE DISTRESS, CALL 911, YOUR LOCAL
POLICE OR A LOCAL WOMEN'S SHELTER.

INFORMATION ON ABUSE, VIOLENCE AGAINST WOMEN AND DOMESTIC VIOLENCE

LEGAL RESOURCES

National Center for Women and Family Law
799 Broadway, Suite 402
New York, NY 10003
212-674-8200

National Clearinghouse for the Defense of Battered Women
125 S. 9th Street
Philadelphia, PA 19107
215-351-0010

NATIONAL ORGANIZATIONS

Center for the Prevention of Sexual and Domestic Violence
1914 N. 34th St., Suite 105
Seattle, WA 98103
206-634-1903

Family Violence Prevention Fund
Building One, Suite 200
1001 Potrero Avenue
San Francisco, CA 94110
415-821-4553

Family Violence and Sexual Assault Institute
1310 Clinic Drive
Tyler, TX 75701
903-595-6600

National Clearinghouse on Marital and Date Rape
2325 Oak Street
Berkeley, CA 94708
510-524-1582

National Coalition Against Domestic Violence
PO Box 18749
Denver, CO 80218
303-839-1852

National Coalition Against Sexual Assault
PO Box 21378
Washington, DC 20009
202-483-7165

National Council on Child Abuse and Family Violence
1155 Connecticut Avenue NW, Suite 400
Washington, DC 20036
202-429-6695
800-422-4453 (referrals regarding child abuse)
800-537-2238 (referrals regarding spouse/partner abuse)
800-221-2681 (referrals for counseling)

National Organization for Victim Assistance
1757 Park Road NW
Washington, DC 20010
202-232-6682 (counseling and business)
800-879-6682 (information and referrals)

National Victim Center
2111 Wilson Boulevard, Suite 300
Arlington, VA 22201
703-276-2880 (main office)
800-877-3355 (referrals)

Rape Crisis Center Hotline
Washington, DC
202-333-7273
This number will provide access to a national directory that will provide information about organizations in your area.

STATE COALITIONS AGAINST DOMESTIC VIOLENCE

Alabama

Alabama Coalition Against Domestic Violence
PO Box 4762
Montgomery, AL 36101
205-832-4842

Alaska

Alaska Network on Domestic Violence and Sexual Assault
419 6th Street #116
Juneau, AK 99801
907-586-3650

Arizona

Arizona Coalition Against Domestic Violence
2345 E. Thomas, Suite 440
Phoenix, AZ 85016
602-224-9477

Arkansas

Arkansas Coalition Against Violence to Women and Children
7509 Cantrell Road, Suite 213
Little Rock, AR 72207
501-663-4688

California

Central California Coalition on Domestic Violence
619 13th Street
Modesto, CA 95354
209-575-7037

Northern California Coalition Against Domestic Violence
c/o Marin Abused Women's Services
1717 5th Avenue
San Rafael, CA 94901
415-457-2464

Southern California Coalition on Battered Women
PO Box 5036
Santa Monica, CA 90405
213-655-6098

Colorado

Colorado Domestic Violence Coalition
PO Box 18902
Denver, CO 800218
303-573-9018

Connecticut

Connecticut Coalition Against Domestic Violence
135 Broad Street
Hartford, CT 06105
203-524-5890

Delaware

Delaware Coalition Against Domestic Violence
c/o Child, Inc.
Philadelphia Pike
Wilmington, DE 19809
302-762-6110

District of Columbia

District of Columbia Coalition Against Violence
c/o Emergency Domestic Relations
111 F. Street NW
Washington, DC 20001
202-662-9666

Florida

Florida Coalition Against Domestic Violence
PO Box 1201
Winter Park, FL 32790
407-628-3885

Georgia

Georgia Advocates for Battered Women and Children
250 Georgia Avenue SE, Suite 365
Atlanta, GA 30312
404-524-3847

Hawaii

Hawaii State Committee on Family Violence
PO Box 31107
Honolulu, HI 96820
808-595-3900 or 808-532-3804

Idaho

Idaho Network to Stop Violence Against Women
5440 Franklin Boulevard, Suite 201
Boise, ID 83705
208-338-1323

Illinois

Illinois Coalition Against Domestic Violence
937 South Fourth Street
Springfield, IL 62703
217-789-2830

Indiana

Indiana Coalition Against Domestic Violence
c/o YWCA Women's Shelter
605 North 6th Street
Lafayette, IN 47901
317-742-0075

Iowa

Iowa Coalition Against Domestic Violence
Lucas Building, First Floor
Des Moines, IA 50319
515-281-7284

Kansas

Kansas Coalition Against Sexual and Domestic Violence
PO Box 1341
Pittsburg, KS 66762
316-232-2757

Kentucky

Kentucky Domestic Violence Association
PO Box 356
Frankfort, KY 40602
502-875-4132

Louisiana

Louisiana Coalition Against Domestic Violence
PO Box 2133
Baton Rouge, LA 70821
504-389-3001

Maine

Maine Coalition for Family Crisis Services
PO Box 590
Sanford, ME 04073
207-324-1957

Maryland

Maryland Network Against Domestic Violence
167 Duke of Glouchester
Annapolis, MD 21401
410-839-5815

Massachusetts

Massachusetts Coalition of Battered Women's Service Groups
210 Commercial Street
Boston, MA 02109
617-248-0922

Michigan

Michigan Coalition Against Domestic Violence
PO Box 16009
Lansing, MI 48901
517-484-2924

Minnesota

Minnesota Coalition for Battered Women
1619 Dayton Avenue #303
St. Paul, MN 55104
612-646-6177

Mississippi

Mississippi Coalition for Battered Women
PO Box 333
Biloxi, MS 39533
601-435-1968

Missouri

Missouri Coalition Against Domestic Violence
311 Madison
Jefferson City, MO 65101
314-634-4161

Montana

Montana Coalition Against Domestic Violence
104 N. Broadway #406
Billings, MT 59101
406-245-7990

Nebraska

Nebraska Domestic Violence Sexual Assault Coalition
315 S. 9th Street, Suite 18
Lincoln, NE 68508
402-476-6256

Nevada

Nevada Network Against Domestic Violence
2100 Capurro Way, Suite 21-I
Sparks, NV 89431
702-358-1171

New Hampshire

New Hampshire Coalition Against Domestic and Sexual Violence
PO Box 353
Concord, NH 03302
603-224-8893
800-852-3388

New Jersey
New Jersey Coalition for Battered Women
2620 Whitehorse-Hamilton Square Road
Trenton, NJ 08690
609-584-8107

New Mexico
New Mexico State Coalition Against Domestic Violence
c/o La Casa, Inc.
PO Box 2643
Las Cruces, NM 88004
505-526-2819
505-525-3792

New York
New York State Coalition Against Domestic Violence
The Women's Building
79 Central Avenue
Albany, NY 12206
518-432-4864

North Carolina
North Carolina Coalition Against Domestic Violence
PO Box 51875
Durham, NC 27717
919-490-1467

North Dakota
North Dakota Council on Abused Women's Services
418 E. Rosser Avenue, Suite 320
Bismarck, ND 58501
701-255-6240 or 800-472-2911

Ohio

Action Ohio Coalition for Battered Women
PO Box 15673
Columbus, OH 43215
614-221-1255

Ohio Domestic Violence Network
PO Box 5466
Cleveland, OH 44101
216-634-7501

Ohio Domestic Violence Network
65 South Fourth Street, Suite 302
Columbus, OH 43215
614-221-0023 or 800-934-9840

Oklahoma

Oklahoma Coalition on Domestic Violence and Sexual Assault
2200 Classen Boulevard, Suite 1300
Oklahoma City, OK 73106
405-557-1210

Oregon

Oregon Coalition Against Sexual and DomesticViolence
2236 SE Belmont Street
Portland, OR 97214
503-239-4486

Pennsylvania

Pennsylvania Coalition Against Domestic Violence
6400 Flank Drive
Gateway Corporate Center, Suite 1300
Harrisburg, PA 17112
800-932-4632 or 717-545-6400

Puerto Rico

Puerto Rico Coalition Against Domestic Violence
N-11 Calle 11
San Souci
Bayamon, PR 00619

Rhode Island

Rhode Island Council on Domestic Violence
324 Broad Street
Central Falls, RI 02863
401-723-3051

South Carolina

South Carolina Coalition Against Domestic Violence and
Sexual Assault
PO Box 7776
Columbia, SC 29202
803-254-3699
803-581-8313

South Dakota

South Dakota Coalition Against Domestic Violence and
Sexual Assault
PO Box 595
Agency Village, SD 57262
605-698-3947

Tennessee

Tennessee Task Force Against Family Violence
PO Box 120792
Nashville, TN 37212
615-327-0805

Texas

Texas Council on Family Violence
8701 North Mopac Expressway
Suite 405
Austin, TX 78759
512-794-1133

Utah

Citizens Against Physical and Sexual Abuse
PO Box 3617
Logan, UT 84321
801-752-4493

Vermont

Vermont Network Against Domestic Violence and Sexual Assault
PO Box 405
Montpelier, VT 05601
802-223-1302

Virginia

Virginians Against Domestic Violence
2850 Sandy Bay Road, Suite 101
Williamsburg, VA 23185
804-221-0990

Washington

Washington State Coalition Against Domestic Violence
200 W Street SE, Suite B
Tumwater, WA 98501
206-352-4029

West Virginia
West Virginia Coalition Against Domestic Violence
PO Box 85
307 Main Street
Sutton, WV 26601
304-765-2250

Wisconsin
Wisconsin Coalition Against Domestic Violence
1051 Williamson Street
Madison, WI 53703
608-255-0539

Wyoming
Wyoming Self-Help Center
341 East E Street, Suite 135A
Casper, WY 82601
307-235-2814

INFORMATION ON ALCOHOL/NARCOTICS ABUSE

Check your local directory or contact:

Al-Anon Family Group Headquarters
PO Box 182
Madison Square Station
New York, NY 10159
212-254-7230 or 800-344-2666

Alcoholics Anonymous
World Services, Inc.
475 Riverside Drive
New York, NY 10115
212-870-3400

Nar-Anon Family Groups
PO Box 2562
Palos Verdes, CA 909274
213-547-5800

Narcotics Anonymous
PO Box 9999
Van Nuys, CA 91409
818-780-3951

INFORMATION ON CHILD CUSTODY AND SUPPORT SERVICES

Custody

Child Custody Evaluation Services of Philadelphia
PO Box 202
Glenside, PA 19038
215-576-0177

The Joint Custody Association
10606 Wilkins Avenue
Los Angeles, CA 90024
213-475-5352

Support

The Association for Children for Enforcement of Support
723 Phillips Avenue, Suite J
Toledo, OH 43612
800-537-7072

Children of Divorce and Separation
PO Box A
Glenside, PA 19038
800-366-8786

The Children's Foundation
725 15th Street NW, Suite 505
Washington, DC 20005
202-347-3300

Children's Rights Council
220 I Street N.E.
Washington, DC 20002
202-547-6227

Committee for Mother and Child Rights
210 Ole Orchard Drive
Clear Brook, VA 22624
703-722-3652

Find Dad
800-729-6667
A private collection agency that will charge a percentage of the
support if collected. There is no fee if they fail to collect.

Grandparents United for Children's Rights
137 Larkin Street
Madison, WI 53705
608-238-8751

Mothers Without Custody
PO Box 27418
Houston, TX 77227
800-457-6962

National Center for Women and Family Law
(see "Legal Resources")

INFORMATION ON DIVORCE

Legal Services

Check with your state bar association or with:

The American Academy of Matrimonial Lawyers
150 N. Michigan Avenue, Suite 2040
Chicago, IL 60601
312-263-6477

Center for Battered Women's Legal Services
105 Chambers Street
New York, NY 10007
212-434-2277

Other Resources

Clearinghouse on Pensions and Divorce
Pension Rights Center
918 North 16th Street N.W., Suite 704
Washington, DC 20006
202-296-3776

Ex-Partners of Servicemen for Equality
PO Box 11191
Alexandria, VA 22312
703-941-5844

National Center for Women and Retirement Research
Long Island University
Southampton Campus
Southampton, NY 11968
516-283-4809

NOW Legal Defense and Education Fund
99 Hudson Street, 12th Floor
New York, NY 10013
212-925-6635

Parents Without Partners
401 Michigan Avenue
Chicago, IL 60611
312-644-6610

INFORMATION ON EMPLOYMENT

Apprenticeship and Non-Traditional Employment for Women
PO Box 2490
Renton, WA 98056
206-235-2212

Women Work! The National Network for Women's Employment
1625 K Street, Suite 300
Washington, DC 20006
202-467-6346

BIBLIOGRAPHY

Ackerman, Robert J. *Children of Alcoholics*. Simon & Schuster, New York, NY, 1987.

Ackerman, Robert J. *Growing in the Shadow*. Health Communications, Deerfield Beach, FL, 1986.

Ackerman, Robert J. *Let Go and Grow*. Health Communications, Deerfield Beach, FL 1987.

Ackerman, Robert J. *Perfect Daughters*. Health Communications, Deerfield Beach, FL, 1989.

Ackerman, Robert J. *Silent Sons*. Simon & Schuster, New York, NY, 1993.

Al-Anon Family Group. *Al-Anon's Twelve Steps and Twelve Traditions*. Al-Anon Family Group Headquarters, New York, NY, 1981.

Beattie, Melody. *Co-dependent No More*. Harper/Hazelden, New York, NY, 1987.

Blaker, Karen. *Born to Please: Compliant Women/Controlling Men*. St. Martin's Press, New York, NY, 1988.

Bowker, Lee H. *Ending the Violence*. Learning Publications, Holmes Beach, FL, 1986.

Brooks, Cathleen. *The Secret Everyone Knows*. Kroc Foundation, San Diego, CA, 1981.

Coates, M. and Gail Paech. *Alcohol and Your Patient: A Nurse's Handbook*. Addiction Research Foundation, Toronto, Canada, 1979.

Cork, Margaret. *The Forgotten Children*. Addiction Research Foundation, Toronto, Canada, 1969. Minneapolis, MN, 1985.

Gelles, R. J. and D. R. Loeske. *Current Controversies in Family Violence.* Sage Publications, Newbury, CA, 1993.

Gondolf, Edward W. *Man Against Woman: What Every Woman Should Know About Violent Men.* TAB/McGraw, Blue Ridge Summit, PA, 1989.

Gondolf, Edward W. *Battered Women As Survivors.* Lexington Books, New York, NY, 1988.

Gondolf, Edward W. and Robert J. Ackerman. "Validity and Reliability of an 'Adult Children of Alcoholics' Index." *The International Journal of the Addictions* 28(3): 257-269, 1993.

Jones, Ann. *Next Time, She'll Be Dead: Battering and How to Stop It.* Beacon Press, Boston, 1994.

Jones, A. and S. Schechter. *When Love Goes Wrong.* HarperCollins, New York, NY, 1992.

Martin, Del. *Battered Wives.* Volcano Press, New York, NY, 1981.

Morehouse, Ellen. "Working in the School with Children of Alcoholic Parents." *Health & Social Work* Vol 4, No 4, 1979.

National Council on Alcoholism. *Questions for Women Drinkers.* Kansas City, MO.

Reddy, Betty. *Family Questions.* Lutheran General Hospital, Park Ridge, IL, 1979.

Riessman, Frank. "What Makes an Effective Self-Help Group" *Self-Help Reporter* 6, November/December, 1983.

Roy, Maria. *Children in the Crossfire.* Health Communications, Deerfield Beach, FL, 1988.

Statistical Profile of Women Clients. The Gables, Minneapolis, MN, 1985.

Subby, Robert. *Lost in the Shuffle.* Health Communications, Deerfield Beach, FL, 1987.

Walker, Lenore. *The Battered Woman.* Harper and Row, New York, NY, 1979.

Wilson-Schaef, Anne. *Co-dependence: Misunderstood—Mistreated.* Harper and Row, San Francisco, CA, 1986.

About the Authors

Robert J. Ackerman, Ph.D., is Professor of Sociology and Director of the Mid-Atlantic Addiction Training Institute at Indiana University of Pennsylvania. He is a co-founder of the National Association for Children of Alcoholics, author of ten books and numerous research articles. He is a national lecturer, has appeared on shows such as *The Today Show*, *Oprah Winfrey*, *CNN Headline News* and his research has been featured in *Newsweek*. He and his wife, Kimberly, have three children and live in Indiana, Pennsylvania.

Susan E. Pickering, M.A., is the program director of the Family Based Mental Health Program at the Indiana County Guidance Center in Indiana, Pennsylvania. Additionally, she has served as a therapist with the sexual abuse unit in the Cambria County Mental Health Program in Johnstown, Pennsylvania. She has worked as a family violence counselor for the Alice Paul House Women's Shelter in Indiana, Pennsylvania and has extensive experience in leading women's groups. She and her husband, Jerry, have three children and live in Indiana, Pennsylvania.

OTHER BOOKS BY
ROBERT J. ACKERMAN, PH.D.

A Husband's Little Black Book
Silent Sons
Too Old to Cry
Perfect Daughters
Let Go & Grow
Same House, Different Homes
Growing in the Shadow
Recovery Resource Guide
Children of Alcoholics

4718